Financially Free for Life

10 New and Radical Strategies For Your Company's Marketing

by Mary Sommerset

COPYRIGHT AND DISCLAIMER

Mary Sommerset

Published by:
Leader Publishing Worldwide
19 Axford Bay
Port Moody, BC V3H 3R4
Tel: 1 888 294 9151
Fax: 1 877 575 9151
Website: www.noresults-nofee.com

DEDICATION

I would like to dedicate this book to John, who gave me my first break when I started a public relations agency. It was an auspicious beginning to my marketing career.

CONTENTS

Chapter 1 ... Create Added Value in Your Business and Make $1 + 1 = 3$

Chapter 2 ... How to Use Promotions for Increased Sales Immediately

Chapter 3 ... Generating an Unlimited Amount of Leads for Your Business

Chapter 4 ... Use Scripts to Increase Sales Immediately

Chapter 5 ... Profiting Over The Phone

Chapter 6 ... Creating Effective Marketing Material

Chapter 7 ... Profiting from Internet Marketing

Chapter 8 ... How to Use Advertising for Immediate Profits

Chapter 9 ... How to Profit from Direct Mail

Chapter 10 ... Profits Through Building a TEAM

INTRODUCTION

This is the first page, but by opening this book you have already taken an important step towards increasing the success of your business. Congratulations in your quest to enhance your business and marketing skills.

This book is a reflection of my path. From starting a public relations agency to working as a Senior Product Marketing Manager for start-ups, through to working for major corporations, developing entrepreneurial market research operations to Director of Strategic Partnerships with other major corporations. I started this venture to help small businesses grow effectively. Much has become fragmented in our always-on world.

This is the reason I have dedicated my future as a Strategic Marketing Specialist. Since starting my company to provide direction for small business operators, I have been literally overwhelmed with the demand for marketing, structure, accountability and for the need to have small business operators surrounding themselves with someone that cares and to provide a proper and profitable third party perspective.

As you follow the book remember it does not matter what industry nor type of business you operate. What matters is that you grasp the heart of the principles, the underlying lessons and strategies, that can help grow any operation in any category of business imaginable. The best time to start is NOW, not tomorrow, not next week or next year.

Yours in success,
Mary Sommerset

PS. If you would like to arrange a meeting to get a profitable third party perspective on your business, please send an email to msommerset1@gmail.com and we will gladly point you in the right direction.

To learn how to avoid the 3 key mistakes all small business owners make, visit www.smallbusinessrocks.us

1

Create Added Value in Your Business and Make 1 + 1 = 3

The majority of small businesses, like yours, are established in response to market demand for a product or service. Many build their businesses by serving that demand, and enjoy growing profits without putting much effort into long-term planning or marketing.

However, what happens when that demand slows or stops? What happens when the competition sets up shop with a "new and improved" version of your product down the road? How do you keep your offering fresh, while growing and maintaining your client base? The answer is by adding value to your product or service.

Added value is a marketing or customer relations strategy that can take the form of a product, service, which is added to the original offering for free, or as part of a discounted package. It, like all other elements in your marketing toolkit, is designed to attract new customers and retain existing ones. A simple example of added value would be if you owned a gift shop, and offered complimentary gift wrapping with every purchase.

If you don't refresh and renew your offering over time, your customers will get bored and be drawn to your competitor. Your employees, too, may become disinterested, and find work elsewhere. Ultimately, both clients and employees will demand additional value to remain loyal – and aren't they the keystones for your business growth?

Can You Add Value to Your Business?

Everyone can add value to their business. Better yet, everyone can *afford* to add value to their business. Adding value doesn't have to blow your marketing budget, or take up hours of your time. There are many ways – big and small – to enhance your business in the eyes of your clients.

The key to adding value is determining what your customers and target market perceive as valuable. You must understand their needs, wants, troubles and inconveniences in order to entice them with solutions through added value products or services. Adding value will add to your profits, but if you don't focus on genuinely helping your clients, you'll have a difficult time attracting them.

Added value works for both product- and service-based businesses. If you offer a service, like hairstyling, try treating your customers with products like a latte while they wait, shampoo samples, or a free conditioning treatment with every sixth visit. If you sell a product, consider offering convenience services – like free shipping or delivery – to make the customer's experience a seamless one. The customer will feel appreciated and their needs will have been taken care of.

Ways to Add Value to Your Business

There are many ways to enhance your offer, depending on your budget and the resources you have access to. You may wish to hold a brainstorming session with your staff to come up with ideas for your business; if your employees are on the front lines, they'll likely have firsthand information about what clients would like to see more of.

Feature Your Expertise

Your intellectual property is a free resource that you have at your disposal to share with your clients. This will make them feel as though they have an inside track. You might want to consider adding it to your business, making it a value-added service.

Expert corner: Supplement your website and newsletter with columns on topics of interest to your customers and of relevance to your service. This will position you as an expert in the marketplace, and give your clients helpful information they won't receive from the competition.

Do It Yourself Tips: This is a great tool for seasonal marketing. Provide your clients with this information on your website, in your newsletters, or on take away note cards in your store or office. Ideas include recipes, craft ideas, gift ideas – all of which are branded with your company logo and contact information, and include your product as an ingredient.

What to Expect Tips: Take your customer through what they should expect in the first few days (weeks) of using your service or product, and how they can make the most of it. This can include assembly instructions, product care and cleaning, or service results (like a 25% increase in business – guaranteed!).

Related + Community Events: Own a store that sells athletic equipment? Post information on your website, in store, and in your newsletter about upcoming races, games, or consumer trade shows. Or simply keep a bulletin in your office of community events and offers that will draw your clients in, and establish itself as a hub in the neighborhood for information.

Offer Convenience Services

Customer service is a dying practice in our high paced culture – use it to your advantage. When done well, it can be the difference between you and the competition, or the deciding factor for a potential repeat client.

Envision the steps involved for a customer to arrive at your store, purchase your offering, and use your product or service. Can you eliminate any of those steps for them? Can you shorten waiting times, or make them more pleasurable? Stepping into your clients' shoes will allow you to determine the most powerful value add for your company. Here are a few ideas:

Free Delivery + Shipping: With clearly established parameters (will you ship your product free to India?), this is a solid value added service that many businesses offer. Free delivery (usually with a purchase over a set amount) is a huge convenience for many people who do not have access to a vehicle, or need help moving large items.

Follow up Services: This works great for computers, appliances and other mechanical or technology-based products. Offer maintenance and service contracts for three time periods; instead of dealing with the manufacturer, customers will rely on you for assistance which brings them back into the store and establishes a relationship of trust.

Gift-Wrapping: A great service to provide – especially for seasonal gifts. This service costs very little, and can have a big impact on your customer's experience.

"While You Wait" Amenities: If you could make your customer feel like a VIP for minimal cost, why wouldn't you? Offering amenities like coffee and treats, free samples and services (wireless internet is a big one) will go a long way.

Comparison-Shopping Tools: Show your customers that you are so sure your product will measure up against the competition, that you'll help them compare.

Establish Complementary Partnerships

Complementary partnerships with other businesses can take you a long way toward adding value for your customer, and generating new business. Just like a joint testimonial mailing, the power (and convenience) of referral business is immense.

Build a web of associates: If you're a yoga instructor, carry the cards of your treatment providers (physiotherapists, massage therapists, etc.) to refer your students to. In exchange, your brochure or card is posted in their offices. This works for automotive repair, esthetics, consultants and other service providers. Customers will trust referrals received by their existing service providers, and feel taken care of by a reputable community of experts.

Establish partnerships with financial incentives: This is one that has your interests in mind as well as your customers'. In addition to establishing a complementary partnership with a related associate, establish an incentive structure where each of you are compensated for your referrals. For example, if you refer a client to a furniture store after they've purchased a mattress from you, and they buy a bed frame, your associate will pay you a portion of the sale – and vice versa.

Location-based partnerships: Consider creating partnerships with the businesses around you – even if your products and services don't appear to be related. Shopping malls do this all the time with value coupon books that customers must purchase for $5 to $20 dollars. These partnerships and incentives will keep the customer spending money in the area, which is good for everyone's bottom line.

Packages + Bundles

Packaging and bundling products and services is one of the most popular methods of adding value. Clients perceive the bundles as having a higher value than the sum of the individual items – or as receiving something for free.

Cleverly packaged and named bundles can spark interest and revive your products in the eyes of your customers. Remember to always give the offers an end date or provide a limited number to create a sense of scarcity and urgency and to prevent this strategy from going stale.

Intuitive product bundles: Package independent related products together, and give them a reduced price or name. For example, this could be selling an extra pair of running socks with new running shoes. Remember the convenience of starter kits – package everything your customer will need to begin a new activity – painting, camping, running, etc. – in a bundle for simple buying decisions.

Package your upsell: This can also be called a chain of purchasing. It includes the products or services your client will need to use your product or service. Won't they need leather protector for their new boots? If they've run out of oil paints, how's their supply of brushes, acrylics or canvases? By packaging these clearly related products together, you are making their shopping experience faster and more convenient.

Offer a Customer Loyalty Program

There are a number of ways to structure your rewards and loyalty program, depending on the type of business and level of technological resources available to you. Customer loyalty programs have a huge advantage – they help build your database of customer information and in most cases allow you to view and analyze purchasing patterns. Here are the most popular:

Every 6th (or 10th) Visit on Us: This works well for business that rely on repeat visits from their customers – like hair salons, coffee shops, auto maintenance, etc. Customers receive a card with store information on the front, and space for stamps or initials on the back. Remember that while

10 is a nice even number, it may be too far in the future for some customers (especially for services that are three to six weeks apart). The idea of six visits is more manageable.

Rewards Dollars: This is the Canadian Tire model. For every dollar your customer spends in store, they receive a small portion back in store credit (i.e., Canadian Tire money). The store credit is in the form of printed dollars, branded with your company logo and contact information, and serves as a reminder each time a client opens their wallet.

Rewards Points: Another common value-add strategy is a rewards points system. Most grocery stores use this incentive, as well as credit card companies. This works the same as rewards dollars, where a certain number of points are accumulated based on each dollar spent in store. Points can then be spent in store, or on products you have brought in for "rewards points holders" only. This strategy also allows you to feature products with "extra points value" instead of discounting prices.

Membership Amenities: Instead of points or dollars, you can offer VIP treatment for members, when they sign up for or purchase a membership. This may include occasional discounts, but is primarily centered around perks like "while you wait" amenities, skipping the line, free delivery, etc. You can also produce membership cards.

2

How to Use Promotions for Increased Sales Immediately

Promotion and revenue go hand in hand. No matter how long you've been in business, or what kind of company you have; keeping your product/service in the forefront of the consumer's mind is an ongoing process. You want to be the one they remember when they go to buy that hair product or need to get their car fixed.

In simple terms, promotion is about communicating who your company is and enticing your target audience to purchase your product or service. It showcases the marketing messages you put out into the world, and aims to achieve your marketing objectives.

It's an umbrella term that encompasses any activity that is done for the purpose of "getting your name out there" and creating sales. It is one of the main components that make up a marketing plan.

Think big shots like Coca Cola and Microsoft no longer have promotional campaigns? On the contrary, in order to stay at the top of their fields they devote a great deal of energy to promotion; and they keep it going regularly.

If you aren't going to the public, but waiting for them to come to you, you're only creating a one way stream of revenue. In this day and age promotion is a cornerstone of success in business.

Why Everyone Needs to Promote Their Business

We've been discussing how essential marketing plans – and proactive strategies in general - are to success in business. Doing so paints the picture of your company's vision. It forces you to ask yourself what your product/service is all about, and how it will meet your target market's need? The groundwork is laid, but how are you going to communicate this with them? This is where promotion comes into the picture....

You can have the best product in the world....but if the world doesn't know about it, it's not doing anyone any good!

"Getting your name out there" is how you are going to create a strong impression in the minds of your potential customers. One way to get into this style of thinking is to see everything you do as a way to do just that. Sure there are standard methods of promotion which can be very useful, but when you "think outside the box" it can really give you an edge against the competition.

The ways of promotion are endless; all you have to do is get yourself into that mind-set. Once you start thinking like the customer, you'll start to understand what THEY want, and then the opportunities of how to provide it, as well as how to let them know about it, shine through.

Brand Awareness

In a marketplace that is full of variety for consumers to choose from, maintaining a presence and reputation amongst all the other brands and products is essential. This is a term called brand awareness, which really just means getting your company and its product/service known, by repetitive exposure of your marketing messages and logo to the public. Promotion is what allows you to achieve this. It also creates interest and curiosity around your product/service.

Consistent Promotion

Equally important to promoting yourself in general, is promoting on a consistent basis. The effectiveness of doing it suffers if you don't commit to it on a frequent basis. This doesn't have to cost a lot of money, there are plenty of cost-effective methods to choose from.

The goal is to "touch base" with the public. If they gain some brand awareness and then you disappear for a while they'll forget about you, "out of sight, out of mind". If and when you start putting your promotional communications out there it will take a while to catch on again, and plus it looks inconsistent. And as we all know by this point, the key to success in marketing is consistency!

Promotional Strategies

Self-Promotion or Networking

Building relationships is not only the foundation of a success in social situations, but also success in business situations. The two go hand in hand, meaning every situation is a chance to make a potential sale.

Some people feel awkward about showcasing themselves, but no one believes in your product/service more than you do. People sense that genuine enthusiasm and it instills them with confidence. Effective promotion begins with how you promote yourself as an individual.

The key is not to make it the only reason for networking, or at the very least not to let it come across that this is the only reason.

A casual way to create an opportunity to discuss your company is to find out about the other person first. This creates a connection and people are always flattered when you inquire about them. It also gives you the opportunity to learn about their needs and desires. Look for clues of how you could relate your product/service to help them in their life.

When it comes to discussing what "you do for a living" they will be more open to receive your enthusiastic promotion. Even if they don't currently have a need for your product/service they are likely to either keep it in mind for the future, and/or pass that information along to friends and family.

This is how you create a buzz, and the beauty of "word of mouth" is born.

Marketing Promotion

This is used to reach a large number of people simultaneously.

One of the major advantages of using some of these methods is the organic creation of a "brand" for your company. When the messages you are putting out there are consistent, and you provide a product or service of consistent quality, it starts to "make a name" for itself.

For example, Nike doesn't need to write lengthy description of what its products are because they have spent so much effort promoting themselves in the past. Now when you see their little "swoosh" logo, you know which company is being mentioned.

It's pretty hard to achieve that by going door to door talking to your neighbors. Using some of the standard promotion methods to showcase your logo, and expose your company's promotional messages gets you known a whole different level.

Here are some examples of simple and cost-effective promotions:

- **Get your business card into as many hands as possible.** Visit friends and family and leave a small stack of business cards with them to give to others. This can create a tremendous trickle-down effect.

- **Have your company logo professionally painted on your vehicle**

- **Be your own billboard.** Have some shirts printed with you company's info on them and sport one when you're running errands or doing leisure activities. Why not even get a few more made so that friends and family can act as a promo team….free of charge!?

- **Write an article on your area of expertise and submit it to a trade magazine or industry newsletter**. Be sure to include your company's contact information at the bottom.

- **Join a few professional associations and attend meetings and functions as an opportunity to network**

- **Always keep business cards on hand, and give them out throughout the day**

- **Put up flyers on public notice boards/community boards and in related businesses. You can even hand them out on the street!**

Types of Promotions

As previously discussed, you know that promotion is any form of communication regarding your product/service or company. This section discusses the variety of standard promotional methods you can use.

If possible, using a variety of these different types enables you to reach your target market in multiple ways; and since the messages you're putting forward are consistent, this creates a greater impact.

Advertising

This is any form of communication that you pay for. It comes across through another source, but is understood that the message comes from what your company wants the public to know about them.

The following outlets are standard methods of advertising:

- Broadcast: Radio, television, internet
- Outdoor: Billboards, bus shelters and even buses themselves
- Print: Programs for event, newspaper/magazines, trade journals

While advertising is projected to the general public, exposing everyone to your message, you want to ensure that you are targeting a specific market. Its effectiveness is easily lost if you are not choosing an outlet that is accepted or used by the group you're selling to. Getting it out there is not enough, it has to make sense.

For example, if you run ads for your new brand of beer on the health and wellness TV station, your sales likely won't be as high as if you aired it during the evenings in between reality TV shows.

Marketing Collateral

This method is often confused with advertising, however it is self-promotion in the fact you don't use any other source to help you get your message across.

Below are commonly used examples:

- Business Cards
- Brochures
- Newsletters
- Flyers
- Posters

Public Relations

This is exposure to your company, and/or product/service that comes from a 3rd party – the media. To maintain the legitimacy of the information portrayed in this way you cannot pay for this exposure.

It comes instead by developing positive relationships with people within the media channels. When they understand your company vision, or product potential, you can work together to create communication to the public.

A good way to create a positive image of your company is to sponsor an event which gives back to the community. Then you would want to call up your buddy Jim at the local newspaper or Sally at your town's popular radio station, and chances are they'll help you promote it. It's a nice two way stream because as part of their job they are always looking for stories that will appeal to the public. And now here you are doing something that shows social awareness and involvement.

Traditional Sales

This method of promotion refers to yourself, a member of your sales team, or a retailer communicating about you product/services in a one to one or small group situation.

Examples include:

- Demonstrations/presentations
- Door-to-door
- Telemarketing

Sponsorship

This is a way to get exposure by affiliating yourself with another organization. You would offer financial support to this company's event, and in turn they would mention you when promoting their event.

You can use sponsorship in many ways. You can use it to create a positive image, by supporting an event that is important to everyone, e.g. Weekend to End Breast Cancer. Alternatively, it works well when you support a company whose product/service is related to you own, e.g. if you are a shoe company you could sponsor a local 10 km race.

Sales Promotion

Not to be confused with the word promotion itself; sales promotion is the action of offering incentives to entice people to try your product/service. These methods are often used to offer a "taster" of your product or service. They serve as a way of bringing in new clients, who you may not have reached without this bait.

It is also a way of attracting customers from your competitors; who may try your similar product/service because of the low rate, and then be "won over" by the quality of your product/service.

The idea is to make the consumers "an offer they can't refuse".

It is often used for a short time; but if long-term goals are set, and the sales promotion is well planned/ executed with them in mind, it can bring success on this level too.

Use sales promotion(s) in the short-term if you're looking to:

- Match the competition
- Move inventory
- Create cash flow

Use sales promotion(s) in the long-term if you're looking to:

- Create additional revenue or market share
- Increase the size of your target market
- Create a positive experience with the product/service
- Enhance product value and brand power

By this point I'm sure you're dying to know, what are these tools I can use to achieve such great things? Well they are things that we see every day when out in the marketplace. Examples:

1. Coupons – discounted prices are always appealing
2. Gift with purchase offers – to appeal to the "I get more than I'm paying for" mentality
3. Sweepstakes/Contests – you get a chance to win with every purchase
4. Free Samples – there's no risk involved, you know what you're buying
5. Specialties – free gifts used as a reminder items (carry your branding/logo)
6. Rebates – get money back if you mail in form
7. Group Discounts
8. Frequent User Incentives – e.g. Get your 7th coffee free after purchasing 6. This is a way to encourage customer loyalty
9. Give-Aways (e.g. Baseball caps or mugs with your logo) – now the public's doing your promoting for you

10. "Early Bird Rates" - this is useful if you are trying to get people to sign up for something, e.g. If you sign-up for this workshop before Oct. 14th the cost is $150.00, after that date it's $180
11. Guarantees – If you're not satisfied with your purchase you can return it for a refund

Packaging

Making sure that the container for your product is appealing, and that it offers the same message as the rest of your promotional efforts is essential. What good is going through all the planning to create a wonderful promotional campaign if a) when the customer gets the product or goes to buy it doesn't draw them in or b) they can't find it because the design fails (e.g. the company or product name is too small or gets lost behind lots of artsy filler).

Customer Service

Now let's say you don't have a product, but a service instead. Even if you are a small business you may have a few employees. It's important that all of the members of your team display a unite front, and communicate the promotion of your service in a consistent manner. And if what your company offers involves these employees providing it for the customer, it is especially important that there is a standard level of service. This is what helps build your brand.

Direct Mail

This involves sending out promotional materials addressed to specific individuals. This has become an increasingly popular method of promotion over the last five years.

There are even sources from whom you can buy databases of companies/individuals within your industry, allowing you to send your communication efforts to the people who are the most likely to need your product/services.

Personalizing the promotional materials you send out the response rates increases the "call to action" (specific result you're trying to achieve). The response rates are higher because people by nature are more inquisitive when they see something with their name on it, rather than what may just be perceived as a general flyer.

Trade Shows

Your product or service might be one that is suited to exhibiting at a trade show attended by your target audience. Trade shows are typically one- or two- day events that allow businesses to set up exhibits or booths showcasing their products or capabilities.

Choosing a Strategy

So with all these options, how do you decide which types of promotions will be the most effective, and will give you the most "bang for your buck"?

Keep these two things in mind:

Research is crucial. This means studying your target market; as well as the competition. Check out a trade magazine to see how they are marketing similar products/services.

A little creativity can go a long way. Think outside the box, and put your own spin on things. In such an environment that's saturated with so many marketing messages, doing something out of the ordinary will catch consumer attention, make you stand out and give you an edge on the competition.

Planning Your Promotions

Like anything in life, and especially in marketing; a well thought out plan is the starting point from which great successes arise. Just as it is necessary to write a general marketing plan; in order to assess your current situation, where you want to go and what it will look like when you get there; the same must be done to get a clear vision of what you want to achieve from your promotional efforts – your promotional campaign.

What is a promotional plan?

A promotional plan is an outline of the ways you're going to promote your product/service to achieve your marketing goals. The promotional plan is only one component of an overall marketing plan, yet it often gets mistaken however for the marketing plan, as it outlines where most of the marketing budget will go.

What do you want to achieve from your promotional efforts?

This is where you would discuss your goals. It is very important to remember that the goals of your promotional efforts are geared to achieve the goals that were set in your marketing plan. Just like the goals in the marketing plan need to focus on achieving the overall objectives of your company.

You want to be as specific as possible here. Just like you don't want to try and be everything to everyone - in terms of your product in the marketplace, you don't want to try and achieve every marketing goal you set at once. Really focus on what you're trying to achieve, whether it be results in the short-term, or paving the way for long-term success. Then just ensure that those are the marketing goals you're working from.

Remember that in order to know whether your efforts have been successful; you have to think in measurable terms from the goal setting phase. By comparing the following two goals it is clear to see which one will be more effective. Goal A = Increase of customers from implementing our new "return business rate". VS Goal B = Increased the repeat customer base by 20%, by year's end, as a result of the newly implemented "return business rate" program.

What message or image do you want to communicate?

You want to make sure that your customers are continually getting the same impression of your product/service, and your company as a whole. To ensure this happens as often as possible, you want to carefully choose what you want to convey.

Then, make sure all the forms of promotion you take lead back to these core communication messages. This is a similar concept to how your promotional efforts need to correspond with your marketing goals and your marketing goals need to correspond to your company goals.

In our environment we are continually surrounded by messages from different companies. They reach us on deeper levels than we realize. For this reason it is so important to maintain consistency in what and how you are communicating with your target market. The idea is that they get the same message so often that they don't even need to distinguish where or how they got it, it just becomes their association with what you are promoting.

This can only be achieved if you don't have conflicting messages. For example, if your packaging focuses on being environmentally friendly, your advertising campaign is about the great value for money of your product and your press releases discuss the health benefits the consumer is confused. What are you trying to provide me? All these different messages conflict in their minds and they are left felling confused, rather than compelled to buy/try your product.

What tools are you going to use to get your message across and achieve your goals?

The varieties of methods you can use to promote your product/services are limited only by your creativity.

What needs to be done for the plan to come into effect?

This is where you look at logistics. Things to think about:

- What kinds of companies will you need to research? (e.g. media, printing, design)
- When does the campaign need to be "up and running?"
- Will all your promotional efforts begin simultaneously, or will they be staggered?
- If you have staff, who will be responsible for what?

How much is it likely to cost to put these promotional efforts in place?

You need to consider how much your promotional vision will cost. And of course, going hand in hand with that is; how much do you have to spend?

One thing to keep in mind is whether or not the need for your product/service changes throughout the year. For example, if you sell snowshoes, this is a seasonal business, and you are not going to need to allot any of your budget toward promoting in the summer.

How will I know if I've achieved my goals? And how will I make sure to keep achieving them?

Having a maintenance plan for monitoring your promotional efforts is a key step; and should not to be overlooked. It ties into the idea of making sure that you're working toward measurable goals. If you don't have a specific result in mind, how do you know when/if you've achieved your goal?

Ways to discover which of your promotional efforts are most effective:

Customers: Your customers are the greatest source you have. After all, your efforts are aimed to appeal to them, so find out which of your promotional activities worked, by asking: "how did you hear about our product/service?" This is the best measure of success you could ask for…and it's free!

Retailers: If you are selling your product via someone else's store, make sure to connect with them regularly to see how things are going. They are an eye-witness to how your product fares against the competition. Find out what they notice in terms of customer perception of your product.

They will also be a different source of feedback than that which comes directly from the customer. They may be privy to information a customer wouldn't tell you, and will likely know all about the praise and/or complaints. So be sure to check in with questions such as: "have they noticed customers picking up your brochures or business cards you left at their store"?

Keep a notebook of comments, feedback and advice from these sources. By referring back to the info you have received by simply seeking this feedback; you can assess which promotional method is bringing in the most sales, and then put more of your efforts and marketing budget toward it in the future.

Promotion Plan Steps

1. Go through the different types of promotional methods and determine their strengths and weaknesses

2. Determine the combination of promotion methods you want to implement

3. Decide which of the goals in your marketing plan you want to achieve with your promotional campaign

4. Look at how much money you have in the budget to allot to promotion

5. Decide what percentage of the budget will go to which method of promotion

6. Determine which messages (aspects) your company and its product/service you want to promote

7. Launch your promotional campaign when all the steps of planning (section D) have been completed

8. Evaluate the results of your promotional efforts

3

Generating an Unlimited Amount of Leads for Your Business

Where do your customers come from?

Most people would probably choose advertising as an answer. Or referrals. Or direct mail campaigns. This may seem true, but it's not really accurate.

Your customers come from leads that have been turned into sales. Each customer goes through a two-step process before they arrive with their wallets open. They have been converted from a member of a target market, to a lead, then to a customer.

So, would it not stand to reason then, that when you advertise or send any marketing material out to your target market, that you're not really trying to generate customers? That instead, you're trying to generate leads.

When you look at your marketing campaign from this perspective, the idea of generating leads as compared to customers seems a lot less daunting. The pressure of closing sales is no longer placed on advertisements or brochures.

From this perspective, the **general purpose of your advertising and marketing efforts is then to generate leads from qualified customers.** Seems easy enough, doesn't it?

Where Are Your Leads Coming From?

If I asked you to tell me the top three ways you generate new sales leads, what would you say?

- Advertising?
- Word of mouth?
- Networking?
- ...don't know?

The first step toward increasing your leads is in understanding how many leads you currently get on a regular basis, as well as where they come from. Otherwise, how will you know when you're getting more phone calls or walk-in customers?

If you don't know where your leads come from, start *today*. Start asking every customer that comes through your door, "how did you hear about us?" or "what brought you in today?" Ask every customer that calls where they found your telephone number, or email address. Then, *record the information for at least an entire week.*

When you're finished, take a look at your spreadsheet and write your top three lead generators here:

1. _____

2. _____

3. _____

From Lead to Customer: Conversion Rates

Leads mean nothing to your business unless you convert them into customers. You could get hundreds of leads from a single advertisement, but unless those leads result in purchases, it's been a largely unsuccessful (and costly) campaign.

The ratio of leads (potential customers) to transactions (actual customers) is called your conversion rate. Simply divide the number of customers who actually purchased something by the number of customers who inquired about your product or service, and multiply by 100.

 # transactions / # leads x 100 = % conversion rate

If, in a given week, I have 879 customers come into my store, and 143 of them purchase something, the formula would look like this:

[143 (customers) / 879 (leads)] x 100 = 16.25% conversion rate

What's Your Conversion Rate?

Based on the formula above, you can see that the higher your conversion rate, the more profitable the business.

Your next step is to determine you own current conversion rate. Add up the number of leads you sourced in the last section, and divide that number into the total transactions that took place in the same week.

Write your conversion rate here:

_____.

Quality (or Qualified) Leads

Based on our review of conversion rates, we can see that the number of leads you generate means nothing unless those leads are being converted into customers.

So what affects your ability (and the ability of your team) to turn leads into customers? Do you need to improve your scripts? Your product or service? Find a more competitive edge in the marketplace?

Maybe. But the first step toward increasing conversion rates is to evaluate the leads you are currently generating, and make sure those leads are the right ones.

What are Quality Leads?

Potential customers are potential customers, right? Anyone who walks into your store or picks up the phone to call your business could be convinced to purchase from you, right? Not necessarily, but this is a common assumption most business owners make.

Quality leads are the people who are the most likely to buy your product or service. They are the qualified buyers who comprise your target market. Anyone might walk in off the street to browse a furniture store – regardless of whether or not they are in the market for a new couch or bed frame. This lead is solely interested in browsing, and is not likely to be converted to a customer.

A quality lead would be someone looking for a new kitchen table, and who specifically drove to that same furniture because a friend had raved about the service they received that month. **These are the kinds of leads you need to focus on generating.**

How Do You Get Quality Leads?

- **Know your target market.** Get a handle on who your customers are – the people who are most likely to buy your product or service. Know their age, sex, income, and purchase motivations. From that information you can determine how best to reach your specific audience.

- **Focus on the 80/20 rule.** A common statistic in business is that 80% of your revenue comes from 20% of your customers. These are your star clients, or your ideal clients. These are the clients you should focus your efforts on recruiting. This is the easiest way to grow your business and your income.

- **Get specific.** Focus not only on who you want to attract, but how you're going to attract them. If you're trying to generate leads from a specific market segment, craft a unique offer to get their attention.

- **Be proactive**. Once you've generated a slew of leads, make sure you have the resources to follow up on them. Be diligent and aggressive, and follow up in a timely manner. You've done to work to get them, now reel them in.

Get More Leads from Your Existing Strategies

Increasing your lead generation doesn't necessarily mean diving in and implementing an expensive array of new marketing strategies. Marketing and customer outreach for the purpose of lead generation can be inexpensive, and bring a high return on investment.

You are likely already implementing many of these strategies. With a little tweaking or refinement, you can easily double your leads, and ensure they are more qualified.

Here are some popular ways to generate quality leads:

Direct Mail to Your Ideal Customers

Direct mail is one of the fastest and most effective ways to generate leads that will build your business. It's a simple strategy – in fact, you're probably already reaching out to potential clients through direct mail letters with enticing offers.

The secret to doubling your results is to craft your direct mail campaigns specifically for a highly targeted audience of your *ideal* customers.

Your ideal customers are the people who will buy the most of your products or services. They are the customers who will buy from you over and over again, and refer your business to their friends. They are the group of 20% of your clients who make up 80% of your revenue.

Identify your ideal customers

Who are your ideal customers? What is their age, sex, income, location and purchase motivation? Where do they live? How do they spend their money? Be as specific as possible.

Once you have identified who your ideal customers are, you can begin to determine how you can go about reaching them. Will you mail to households or apartment buildings? Families or retirees? Direct mail lists are available for purchase from a wide range of companies, and can be segregated into a variety of demographic and sociographic categories.

Craft a special offer

Create an offer that's too good to refuse – not for your entire target market, but for your ideal customer. How can you cater to their unique needs and wants? What will be irresistible for them?

For example, if you operate a furniture store, your target market is a broad range of people. However, if you are targeting young families, your offer will be much different than one you may craft for empty-nesters.

Court them for their business

Don't stop at a single mail-out. Sometimes people will throw your letter away two or three times before they are motivated to act. Treat your direct mail campaign like a courtship, and understand that it will happen over time.

First send a letter introducing yourself, and your irresistible offer. Then follow up on a monthly basis with additional letters, newsletters, offers, or flyers. Repetition and reinforcement of your presence is how your customer will go from saying, "who is this company" to "I buy from this company."

Advertise for lead generation

Statistics show that nearly 50% of all purchase decisions are motivated by advertising. It can also be a relatively cost effective way of generating leads.

We've already discussed the importance of ensuring your advertisements are purpose-focused. The general purpose of most advertisements is to increase sales – which starts with leads. However ads that are created solely for lead generation – that is, to get the customers to pick up the phone or walk in the store – are a category of their own.

Lead generation ads are simply designed and create a sense of curiosity or mystery. Often, they feature an almost unbelievable offer. Their purpose is not to convince the customer to buy, but to contact the business for more information.

As always, when you are targeting your ideal audience, you'll need to ensure that your ads are placed prominently in publications that audience reads. This doesn't mean you have to fork over the cash for expensive display ads. Inexpensive advertising in e-mail newsletters, classifieds, and the yellow pages are very effective for lead generation.

Here are some tips for lead generation advertising:

Leverage low-cost advertising

Place ads in the yellow pages, classifieds section, e-mail newsletters, and online. If your target audience is technology savvy, consider new forms of advertising like Facebook and Google Adwords.

Spark curiosity

Don't give them all the information they need to make a decision. Ask them to contact you for the full story, or the complete details of the seemingly outrageous offer.

Grab them with a killer headline

Like all advertising, a compelling headline is essential. Focus on the greatest benefits to the customer, or feature an unbelievable offer.

Referrals and host beneficiary relationships

A referral system is one of the most profitable systems you can create in your business. The beauty is once it's set up, it often runs itself.

Customers that come to you through referrals are often your "ideal customers." They are already trusting and willing to buy. This is one of the most cost-effective methods of generating new business, and is often the most profitable. These referral clients will buy more, faster, and refer further business to your company.

Referrals naturally happen without much effort for reputable businesses, but with a proactive referral strategy you'll certainly double or triple your referrals. Sometimes, you just need to ask!

Here are some easy strategies you can begin to implement today:

Referral incentives

Give your customers a reason to refer business to you. Reward them with discounts, gifts, or free service in exchange for a successful referral.

Referral program

Offer new customers a free product or service to get them in the door. Then, at the end of the transaction, give them three more 'coupons' for the same free product or service that they can give to their friends. Do the same with their friends. This ongoing program will bring you more business than you can imagine.

Host-beneficiary relationships

Forge alliances with non-competitive companies who target your ideal customers. Create cross-promotion and cross-referral direct mail campaigns that benefit both businesses.

Lead Management Systems

Once your lead generation strategies are in place, you'll also need a system to manage incoming inquiries. You'll need to ensure you receive enough information from each lead to follow up on at a later date. You'll also need to create a system to organize that information, and track the lead as it is converted into a sale.

Gathering Information from Your Leads

Here is a list of information you should gather from your leads. This list can be customized to the needs of your business, and the type of information you can realistically ask for from your potential customers.

- Company Name
- Name of Contact
- Alternate Contact Person
- Mailing Address
- Phone Number
- Fax Number

- Cell Phone
- Email Address
- Website Address
- Product of Interest
- Other Competitors Engage

Lead List Management Methods:

Once you have gathered information from your lead, you'll need a system to organize their information and keep a detailed contact history.

The simplest way to do this is with a database program, but you can also use a variety of hard copy methods.

Electronic Database Programs

- High level of organization available
- Unlimited space for notes and record-keeping
- Data-entry required
- Examples include: MS Outlook, MS Excel, Maximizer
- Customer Relationship Management Software

Index Cards

- Variety of sizes: 3x5, 4X6 or 5X8
- Basic contact information on one side
- Notes on the other side
- Easy to organize and sort

Rolodex System

- Maintain more contacts than index card system
- Easily organized and compact
- Basic contact information on one side
- Notes on the other side
- Can keep phone conversation and purchase details

Notebook

- Best if leads are managed by a single person
- Lots of room for notes
- Inexpensive
- Difficult to re-organize
- Best for smaller lists

Business Card Organizer

- Best for small lists – under 100
- Limited space for notes
- No data entry required
- Rolodex-style, or clear binder pages

4

Use Scripts to Increase Sales Immediately

What do playbooks, prompts, guides and scripts all have in common?

They are all popular tools that dictate or guide human behavior toward a desired outcome.

Playbooks help coaches tell sports teams specifically how to play the game to overcome an opponent. Prompts help to kick-start writers and other creative professionals when stuck in a rut. Guides provide a series of instructions so that a person or team of people can complete or implement a specific task. Film scripts tell actors how to act for a particular part.

If you're in the business of sales, you also know about sales scripts. Sales scripts are tools that guide salespeople during interactions or conversations with potential customers.

A large number of businesses use scripts, either as a way of maintaining consistency amongst a sales team, training new salespeople, or enhancing their sales skills. They may have a single script, or several, and may change their scripts regularly, or use the same one for years.

What most businesses overlook, however, is that the sales script is a living, breathing, changing member of their sales team. They may be internal documents, but they deserve just as much time and effort as your marketing collateral.

Do You Really Need a Script?

The short answer is yes. You absolutely need a script for any and every customer interaction you and your salespeople may find yourselves in.

Sure, countless business owners and salespeople work every day without a script. If you own your own business, chances are you're already a pretty good salesperson. But if you are not using scripts, you're only working at half of your true potential – or half of your potential earnings.

Scripts don't have to be "cheesy" or read verbatim. They act as a map for your sales process, and provide prompts to trigger your memory and keep you on track. How many times have you made a cold call that didn't work out the way you wanted it to? Scripts dramatically improve the effectiveness and efficiency of your sales processes.

A comprehensive set of scripts will also keep a level of consistency amongst your salespeople and the customer service they provide your clients.

Once scripts are written, memorized, and rehearsed, they become like film scripts; the salesperson can breathe their own life and personality into the conversation, while staying focused on the call's objectives.

Why Your Scripts Aren't Working

If you a currently using scripts in your business, are they working? Are they as effective as they could possibly be? How do you know? When was the last time they were reviewed or updated?

Scripts are like any other element of your marketing campaign – they need to be tested and measured for results, and changed based on what is or is not working.

Measure the success of your script based on your conversion rates. Of all the people you speak to and use the script, how many are being converted from leads to sales?

When evaluating your existing scripts, ask yourself the following questions:

How old is this script? What was it written for? Scripts are living, breathing members of your company. They need to be written and rewritten and rewritten again as the needs of your customers change, your product or services change, or as new strategies are implemented.

Does this script address all the customer objections we regularly hear? Every time you hear a customer raise an objection that is not included on the script, add it. The power of your script lies in the ability to anticipate customer concerns, and answer them before they're raised.

Does this script sound the same as the others? Your scripts are part of the package that represents you as a company. There should be a consistent feel or approach throughout your scripts that your customers will recognize and feel confident dealing with.

Is everyone using the script? Who on your team regularly uses these scripts? Just the junior staff? Only the top-performing staff? Make sure everyone is singing from the same song sheet – your customers will appreciate the consistency.

Types of Scripts

Depending on the product or service you offer and the marketing strategies you have chosen, there are countless types of scripts you could potentially prepare for your business,

When you sit down to create your scripts, it would be wise to start by making a list of all the instances you and your staff members interact with your existing or potential customers. Then, prioritize the list from most to least important, and start writing from the top.

Here are some commonly used scripts, and their purposes:

Sales presentation script

Each time you or your sales staff make a presentation, they should be using the same or a slightly modified version of the same script. This script will include sample icebreakers, a presentation on benefits and features of the product or service, and a list of possible objections and responses. These scripts should also help alleviate some of the nervousness or anxiety associated with public speaking.

Closing script

Closing scripts help you do just that: close the sale. This could include a list of closing prompts or statements to get the transaction started. This type of script also includes a list of possible customer objections, and planned responses.

Incoming phone call script

Everyone who calls your business should be treated the same way; consistent information should be gathered and provided to the customer. The person answering the phone should state the company name, department name, and their own name in the initial greeting. This goes for both the main line, and each individual or department extension.

Cold call script

This is one of the most important scripts you can perfect for your business. The cold call script must master the art of quickly getting the attention of the customer, then engaging and persuading them with the benefits of the product or service. The caller needs to establish common ground with the potential customer, and find a way to get them talking through open-ended questions.

Direct mail follow-up script

Scripts for outgoing calls that are intended to follow up on a direct mail piece are essential for every direct mail campaign. They are designed to call qualified leads that have already received information and an offer, and convert them into customers. These scripts should focus on enticing customers to act, and overcoming any objections that may have prevented them from acting sooner.

Market research script

Scripts that are used primarily for the purpose of gathering information should be designed to get the customer talking. A focus on open-ended questions and relationship building statements will help to relax the customer, and encourage honest dialogue.

Difficult customer script

Just like every salesperson needs to practice the sales process, you and your staff also need to practice your ability to handle difficult customers. If you operate a retail business this is especially important, as difficult customers often present themselves in front of other customers. These scripts should help you diffuse the situation, calm the customer down, and then handle their objections.

Creating Scripts

Creating powerful scripts is not a complicated exercise, but it will take some time to complete. Focus on the most vital scripts for your business first, and engage the assistance of your sales staff in drafting or reviewing the scripts.

Your Script Binder

Keep master copies of all of your scripts in one organized place. An effective way to do this is to create a binder, and use tabs to separate each type of script.

You will also want to create a separate tab for customer objections, and list every single customer objection you have ever heard in relation to your product or service. Find a way to organize each objection so you can easily find them – group them by category or separate them with tabs.

Then, list your responses next to each objection – there should be several responses to each objection created with different customer types in mind. A master list of customer objections and responses is an invaluable tool for any business owner, salesperson, and script writer. The more responses you can think of, the better.

Remember, the script binder is never "finished." You will need to make sure that it is updated and added to on a regular basis.

Writing Scripts – Step by Step

Step One: Record What You're Doing Now

If you aren't using scripts – or even if you are – start by recording yourself in action. Use video or audio recording to tape yourself on the phone, in a sales presentation, or with a customer.

Make notes on your body language, word choice, customer reaction and body language, responses to objections, and closing statements.

You may also wish to ask an associate to make notes on your performance and discuss them with you in a constructive fashion.

Step Two: Evaluate What You're Doing Wrong

Take a look at your notes, and ask yourself the following questions:

- How are you engaging the customer?
- Are you building common ground and trust?
- Does what you are saying matter to the customer?
- Is your offer a powerful one?
- What objections are raised?
- How are you dealing with them?
- What objections are you avoiding?
- How natural is your close?
- Are you as effective as you think you can be?

Once you have answered and made notes in response to these questions, make a list of things you need to improve, and how you think you might go about doing so. Do you need to strengthen your closing statements? Do you need to brainstorm more responses to objections? Remember that everyone's script and sales process can be improved.

Step Three: Decide Who the Script is For

So now that you know the elements of your script you need to work on, you can begin drafting your new script, or revising an old one.

The first part of writing a script – or any piece of marketing material – is having a strong understanding of who you are writing it for. Who is your target audience? What does your ideal customer look like? Consider demographic characteristics like age, sex, location, income, occupation and marital status. Be as specific as possible. What are their purchase patterns? What motivates them to spend money?

If you are writing a cold call script, you will need to develop or purchase a list of people who fall into the target market specifics you have established. If you are writing a sales script for in-store customers, then spend some time reviewing what types of customers find their way into your place of business.

You will want to use words that your target audience will not only understand, but relate to and resonate with. Use sensory language that will trigger emotional and feeling responses – *I need this, this will solve that problem, I'll feel better if I have this, etc.*

Step Four: Decide What You Want to Say

There are typically five sections of every script – and there may be more, depending on the type and purpose of script:

1. Engage

- Get their attention or pique their interest
- Establish common ground
- Build trust, be human
- Ask for their time

2. Ask + Qualify

- Take control of the conversation by asking questions
- Focus on open-ended questions that cannot be answered with a "yes" or "no"
- Get the customer talking
- Ask as many questions as you need to get information on the customer's needs and purchase motivations

3. Get Agreement

- Ask closed-ended questions you are sure they will respond with "yes"
- Get them to agree on the benefits of the product or service
- Repeat key points back to the customer to gain agreement

4. Overcome Objections

- Anticipate objections based on customer comments, then refute them
- Make informative assumptions about their thought process, identify with their concern, then refute it using your own experiences
- Repeat concerns back to the customer to let them know you have heard them
- Ask about any remaining objections before you close

5. Close

- Assume that you have overcome all objections, and have the sale
- Ask the customer transactional questions, like delivery timing and payment method
- Be as confident and natural as possible

Step Five: Train Your Staff

Once you have written your company's scripts, you will need to ensure your staff understand and are comfortable using them.

Consider having a team meeting, and use role play to review each of the scripts. This will encourage your salespeople to practice amongst each other, and strengthen their sales skills. Ask them for feedback on the scripts, and make any necessary changes.

You will also need to decide how comfortable you are having your salespeople personalizing the scripts to suit their own styles. Be clear what elements of the script are "company standards" and essential techniques, but also be flexible with your team.

Step Six: Continually Revise

After you have carefully crafted your script, put it to the test. Practice on your colleagues, friends, and family. Get their feedback, and make changes.

Remember that scripts will need to change and evolve as your business changes and evolves, and new products or services are introduced. Keep your script binder on your desk at all times, and continually make changes and improvements to it.

You may also wish to record and evaluate your performance on a regular basis. This is an exercise you could incorporate into regular employee reviews, to use as a constructive tool for staff development.

Script Tips

- Practice anticipating and eliciting real objections – including the ones your customer doesn't want to raise.

- Make the script yours – it should look, feel, and sound like you naturally do, not like you're reading off the page.

- Spend time with the masters. If there is a salesperson you admire in your community, ask to observe them in action. Take notes on their performance, and the techniques they use for success.

- If your script is not successful, ask the customer why not? Even if you don't get the sale, you'll get a new objection you can craft responses to and never get stumped by it again.

- Don't fear objections. Just spend time identifying as many as possible, then practice overcoming them.

- Never stop thinking of responses to customer objections. Each objection could potentially have 30 responses, geared toward specific customer types.

- Anecdotes are persuasive writing tools – use them in your scripts. People enjoy hearing stories, especially stories that relate to them and their experiences, frustrations, and troubles. Let the story sell your product or service for you.

- Include body language in your scripts – it's just as important as your words. Try mimicking your subject's posture, arm position, and seating position. This is proven to create ease and build trust.

- If you only have your voice, use it. Pay attention to tone, language choice, speed, and background noise. You only have sound to establish a trusting relationships, so do it carefully.

- Be confident, and focus on a positive stream of self-talk to prepare for the call or presentation. Confidence sells.

- Spend time on your closing scripts, as they are a critical component of your presentation or phone call. This can be a challenging part of the sales process, so practice, practice, practice.

5

Profiting Over the Phone

For some, the word 'telemarketing' brings up images of rows of people with headsets, all working from a head office in a country far, far away.

Others think of the people who always seem to call the minute they take their first bite of dinner. Some just think it's an old fashioned marketing strategy. While in some cases this may be true, telemarketing is still an important tool for every business – of every size.

What if I were to tell you that you were *already* using telemarketing as a regular part of your business? In fact, telemarketing is re-emerging as a powerful way to generate leads and close sales. Done well, it's also efficient and cost-effective.

Every time the people who work your front end pick up the phone, they're engaging in a telemarketing process. Every time one of your salespeople picks up the phone, they too are engaging in a telemarketing process.

Telemarketing is not just a system for cold calls. It's any type of formal communication between your company and its clients over the phone.

So, now you know that you're already doing it, let's talk about how to turn telemarketing into a profitable marketing strategy for your business.

Telemarketing for Your Business

A common misconception is that telemarketing needs to happen on a broad scale in order to be effective. Pages and pages of potential customers must be cold called on a daily basis. Businesses must hire dozens of staff members to conduct and manage the efforts.

Like I mentioned above, telemarketing is any kind of formal communication that happens between a company and a potential or existing client over the phone. Regardless of the size of your business, you can train you existing staff members to effectively use the telephone to generate more leads and convert more sales.

The benefits of establishing an organized telemarketing system are:

- Instant access. Reach key decision-makers immediately.
- One-on-one interaction. Develop real relationships with empathy and trust.
- Minimal cost. Spend less on sales outreach and research.

Who are the Best Telemarketers?

Success in telemarketing has a lot to do with the personality of your company's representative. Generally, good telemarketers have the following qualities and abilities:

- Energy and enthusiasm

- Positive attitude

- Good phone manner

- Empathy

- Belief in your company and its products

- Strong listening skills

- Ability to think on-the-spot

- Ability to handle objection and rejection

- Good organizational skills

The Telemarketing Process

There are two types of telemarketing: outgoing and incoming. You should have a proactive strategy in place to handle both types.

Remember that your approach to telemarketing must have a clear objective; a clear purpose. What is the purpose of the call (outgoing and incoming)? Is it to inform? Set up an appointment? Establish a need or desire? This will help guide how you handle each type.

Incoming Calls

When a customer calls your business for the first time, you should have a system in place to make a great, customer service-oriented impression. Many of these customers will have seen one of your advertisements, received a direct mail piece, or be responding to any other element of your marketing campaign.

Your telemarketing strategy for incoming phone calls can take the form of:

- An answering service
- Voice mail
- A messaging service
- An order taking system
- An information provision system

The person – or people – who answer incoming calls should be well trained for the role and clearly understand the expectations for handling them. Your receptionist should be trained thoroughly in the products and services you sell so he can answer basic customer questions intelligently. Your team should know how to answer the phone according to your company policy, and have excellent phone manners.

Consider including the following instructions into your incoming telemarketing system or process:

- Answer the phone after two and before four rings
- Have a standard company greeting. Include your company name, as well as the name of the person answering the phone.
- Ensure sufficient customer information is recorded. Determine what information is important to gain from each caller – name, phone number, reason for call, action required, who is responsible for following up
- Do not place anyone on hold for longer than 20 seconds. Instead, take their name and number and have their call returned promptly.

- Establish a short description of your company's process or point of difference at some point during the phone call.
- Always repeat back any information or agreement exchanged.
- Be the last one to hang up.

Outgoing Calls

Outgoing calls are the more challenging aspect of your telemarketing strategy. In this case you are proactively asking your customer for something, as opposed to responding once they've already been convinced to act.

You can use an outgoing telemarketing strategy to:

- Set appointments
- Generate leads
- Make cold calls
- Update databases
- Follow up on direct mail and other campaigns
- Convert leads to sales
- Conduct surveys

Your outgoing phone call needs to engage the person on the other end, and begin to build a relationship based solely on verbal communication (i.e., without the assistance of non-verbal cues and behaviors). Depending on the type of call, you will be seeking to:

- Attract their attention
- Spark their interest, needs, or desires
- Motivate them to act
- Seek agreement

It is essential to the success of your outgoing telemarketing efforts that you create a script for each type of outgoing call your company makes. This will keep you – and your staff – focused on the purpose of the call and give you tools and prompts to keep you on track. We will review scripts for telemarketing later in this chapter.

Here are some simple steps for making your outgoing telemarketing efforts a success:

Know who you are calling

Do your research. Know exactly who it is you need to contact at each company. Is it the manager or vice-president? Owner or CEO? Once you know who you are targeting, you can do some research prior to your phone call, and ensure you call at a time that is convenient. You will want to know a bit about their industry as well as the company and their role within it. If you have served another client in the same industry, let them know.

When you have them on the phone, confirm that the basic information you have is correct (name, title, etc.). If you do not know who the best person to speak to is, ask the receptionist for the name of the person who makes purchasing decisions related to your product.

Be prepared; stay organized

Have all the materials you may need in front of you, and clear your desk of any distractions. Have a notepad handy, and record key elements of the conversation for action or later discussion. Also, keep a record of all the calls you make, and the results of each call. This will prevent you from making duplicate calls, which do not reflect well on your organization, as well as track left messages and the most productive times of the day for outgoing phone calls.

Know why you are calling

Like I mentioned above, your phone calls should be purpose-focused. Are you calling to set up a meeting? Introduce yourself and your products? Get them to try what you have to offer? Keep this clear in your mind and stick to it.

Get past the gatekeeper

To reach busy decision makers, you will have to get past the person who screens unsolicited phone calls: the gatekeeper, assistant, or secretary. Do not assume you will be able to speak to them with the first phone call – it may take two, three, or even seven tries until you are successful. Here are some guidelines for developing a relationship with the gatekeeper:

- Ask for their name and write it down
- Do not underestimate the power of developing a relationship with them
- Get an understanding of their position and responsibilities
- Stay positive and confident

- Never pitch the receptionist on your product
- Once you have developed a relationship, ask them to help you pin the decision-maker down

Be persistent

Persistence pays off – especially when it comes to large potential accounts. You may have to call many times before you can work your way through the gatekeeper, to the person you wish to speak to. Expect this, stay positive, and your persistence will pay off.

Use strong phone skills

You can create a great first impression on the phone when you cultivate great phone communication skills. Pay attention to the tone of your voice, whether or not you are smiling, the pacing of your sentences (slower is better), and general phone manners. Ensure you clearly identify who you are and what company you work for every time you speak to someone new.

Telemarketing Scripts

Scripts are essential to successful telemarketing. You and your employees will benefit having a "plan of action" for every type of phone call that your company makes. This will also ensure that each staff member has a consistent approach, which is part of your branding.

We discussed the importance of scripts and writing scripts earlier in the program, but I encourage you to review the section before you craft your telemarketing scripts.

Here is a list of components you will need to include in your scripts:

Greeting: Opening the Conversation

Your incoming calls should be handled with a consistent, friendly greeting that informs the customer of what company (or department) they've reached and who they're talking to.

Outgoing calls need to engage the customer within the first few moments, just as a headline needs to catch the reader's instant attention. Say just enough to pique their interest and keep them listening, then begin to explain why you are calling.

The opening conversation should be simple and focused on developing a relationship. Ask casual questions and use small talk to put the caller at ease, but don't go on too long. You don't want to appear to be wasting their time.

Reason for your Call

If someone asks why you are calling, tell them. Be up front about why you are calling; clearly state your objectives, then back them up with an explanation that includes benefits to the customer.

You may wish to ask permission before you get into an explanation. Asking, "do you mind if I tell you exactly why I called today?" shows respect for the customer's time, and gives them an opportunity to agree to listen.

You may also wish to outline exactly what you're going to cover during the call. Again, ask them if you can go over this information with them. This will show that you have given the phone call substantial thought, organized your information, and respect their time.

Asking Questions

Information gathering is an essential component of both incoming and outgoing telemarketing. Ask as many questions as possible, and encourage your customer to start talking. This will keep you in control of the conversation. Even if these questions don't relate specifically to the product, your customer will provide firsthand information that you can add to your market research.

For incoming calls, listen to the customer's question, then ask if you can take a moment to ask them some questions before you answer theirs. This will allow you to explain your company's process, ask the customer some qualifying questions, and gain control of the conversation.

You will want to also consider asking questions related to the following topics:

- **Responsibility** – Who is in charge of making the decision? Is it the same person who will be making the purchase?

- **Budget** – How much financial resources are available for your product/service? What is the budget? What influences this number?

- **Timeframe** – When does the customer need the product or service? When will the transaction and delivery process have to be completed by? What is the reason for these deadlines?

- **Competition** – Who else is the customer talking to? What will impact their decision? What aspects are they comparing?

Closed-ended questions

Closed-ended questions are not the best way to get your customer talking, but they do provide information quickly and succinctly. Closed-ended questions are questions that can be answered with one word – usually yes or no.

Open-ended questions

Open-ended questions are just that: they cannot be answered in one word. These are great questions to use for the majority of your telemarketing because they encourage the customer to provide explanations, giving you insight into their needs and opinions.

Obtaining Agreement

At key points throughout the conversation, you will need to ensure you are on the same page as your customer. You will need to find a way to get some feedback from your caller on what you have been saying.

An easy way to do this is to ask them a question you are sure they'll say yes to. Something like, "so as you can see, it's a pretty irresistible offer," or "I'm sure anyone would benefit from using these sprockets in their home."

Encouraging them to agree with you strengthens your argument, and leads directly to the sale. It's a powerful method of persuasion.

Overcoming Objections

This will be the most challenging component of your script – largely because you do not know for sure what your customer's objections are going to be. You will have to think in the moment, and attempt to overcome each objection in a calm, professional way.

Before you pick up the phone, you may wish to brainstorm all potential objections, and think of your ideal response. A simple chart that looks like this will be a helpful tool to refer to during your call:

Potential Objection	Response

Remember to respect the objections as they are raised, and treat each point your customer makes as a legitimate one. Show empathy and relate to what they have to say. Phrases like "I can see how that would be a concern for you…" "I used to think the same thing…" and "Sure, that's completely understandable…" allow you to relate to them, establish common ground, and then share how you overcame your own objections.

Closing with Commitment

Once you have opened the conversation, developed a relationship, asked questions, secured agreement, and overcome objections, all you have to do is close the conversation with a commitment.

The commitment should be your objective for calling, or a step toward that objective. For example, if the purpose of your call was to set up a meeting, ensure that you commit to a time and place before you end the conversation. If your objective is to make a sale, you may have to make a few phone calls or hold a few appointments to achieve that.

Assume that if you have got this far, you have the sale. Be confident, and use phrases like, "How about we meet on this day at this time..." and "Where can I send the product?"

You will want to confirm whatever you have committed to in writing with your customer. If you have set an appointment, send them a quick note to thank them for the phone call, and put the meeting in writing. Remember to be as polite and succinct as possible. Avoid lengthy emails and letters.

Tips for Effective Telemarketing

Communicating with your existing and potential customers over the phone requires a different set of skills than in-person communication. Make sure you choose the best people for this job – when you only have your voice to communicate, you must be extra aware of the impression you give the person on the other line.

Smile

This may seem like a silly point to put at the top of this list, but it is important. Your caller will be able to hear if you are smiling, and interpret your smile as enthusiasm. You will sound more positive, friendly, and open to dialogue. Remember, the person on the other line can hear *everything*, so avoid multi-tasking (drinking, eating, unnecessary typing) when you're on the phone.

Be a good listener

Once you get your customer talking – listen. They will be giving you important insight into their purchase motivations, and their potential objections. Take notes as you listen, and never assume you know what they are going to say. After long periods of speech, check in and repeat back what you have heard to confirm you have heard it properly. Make sure to leave a pause between what they have just said, and what you are about to say. This shows that you have been listening and are not jumping in at your first opportunity.

Call at an optimal time

Knowing who you are calling will ensure that you contact them at the most appropriate time – the time they are most likely to answer you phone call. For example, business owners will need to be reached during business hours. Try to reach them during quiet times – usually first thing in the morning, or right before close. If you are calling consumers, then make your calls in the evening when they are most likely to be home.

Use a familiar tone

You only have your voice to establish a new relationship with a potential customer. The tone you choose is just as important – and has just as much impact – as the words you choose. Use a tone that is friendly and confident, and resembles the way you would speak to your friends.

Be prepared to handle rejection

No matter how targeted your contact list, how amazing your script, how great your approach, rejection is an inevitable part of outgoing telemarketing. Your telemarketers are going to have to become very skilled at handling rejection. In fact, some people will not only reject what you have to say, they'll be rude in doing so. Remember not to take this personally – they could be having a bad day, or just not have enough time to listen to what you have to say. Consider asking to call back at a better time – or just shrug it off.

Be prepared to handle difficult customers

Difficult customers will appear on the other end of the phone line – for both incoming and outgoing calls. This is another inevitability of telemarketing, and business in general. Again, remember not to take what they have to say personally – they just want to air their frustrations and be heard. Listen intently, stay calm, and try to empathize with what they have to say. Never interrupt, use calming language, and record as much as possible about what they are saying. Then, either promise to follow up – allowing yourself to take time to consider how you would like to handle the problem – to try to resolve their issue immediately.

Make the call standing up

When you are standing, you will sound my confident, authoritative, and decisive. Your diaphragm is expanded when you are standing, which will increase the confidence in your voice. Do this for the important phone calls – the big accounts.

Have strong phone manners

Here are some tips for ensuring you have a strong, professional phone presence:

- Ask for the contact by name, not role title
- Use your full name when asked who is calling
- Clearly state your company name
- Tell them why you are calling
- If you do not reach your customer, ask for a more convenient time
- Do not hold, call back instead (your time is valuable, too!)

6

Creating Effective Marketing Material

Your marketing collateral gets sent out in the world to do one thing: act as an ambassador for your product or service, in place of *you*. This may seem like a big job for a piece of paper, but it's a helpful way to think about the materials you create.

When you meet with a potential or existing client, you do a number of things. You make sure you are well prepared with all the information the customer could need. You dress in clothing that is appropriate. You anticipate their needs, and offer a solution to their problems. You may also cater to how they best like to receive information.

Chances are, you wouldn't meet with clients just for the sake of meeting with a client – say, for instance, to show off your new suit. Likewise, you shouldn't create and distribute collateral that is non-essential.

We all know that the biggest challenge for small businesses is the limited number of zeros attached to their marketing budget. Marketing materials can be expensive, and a single, well-produced piece has the ability to devour the entire budget. Given that billion-dollar marketing campaigns fail every day, how can you be sure to make the most of, and be successful with, the dollars you're working within?

The answer? Limit yourself to only the essential items for your individual business, and produce them *well* with the resources you have.

Your Essential Marketing Materials

The easiest way to throw away your marketing budget is to create and produce marketing materials *you don't need.* Since many pieces of collateral are paper-based, this not only leaves you with boxes of extra (outdated) materials, but also takes a huge toll on the environment.

Take some time to determine what marketing materials you do need, and stick to your list. It's easy to want to "keep up with the Joneses" when your competition comes out with a new piece, but remember your focus should be on attracting and retaining a customer base, not matching the competition item for item.

Know your target market. Make sure you have a solid understanding of your customer base. From that knowledge, you can easily determine what the best way is to reach out and communicate with them. Are they a paper-based or techno savvy client group? Do they appreciate being contacted by email or mail? Are they impressed by flashy design, or simple pieces? *How* you communicate is often just as or more important than *what* you communicate.

Pay attention to costs. Do you really need a die-cut business card? Does your flyer absolutely require ink to the edges? Unique touches to marketing collateral can grab a customer's attention, but they can also dramatically increase the cost of production. Keep an eye out during the design process and make strategic choices about graphic elements.

Make mistakes – in small batches. Not sure if that flyer is going to do the trick? Testing out a limited time offer? Small production runs may cost a little more, but you'll avoid collecting boxes of unusable materials. Or, try a split run with type versions of the same piece and see what works best.

Keep the environment in mind. Environmental responsibility is on everyone's mind these days – including your customers. Always question if a particular marketing item can be produced in electronic format. Consider eliminating plastic bags in exchange for cloth ones, printed with your logo; print everything double-sided; send electronic newsletters; use your website to communicate; and, use recycled paper and envelopes when you can.

Brainstorm your wish list. Create a list of desired marketing materials, and ignore expenses, clients, or any other constraint. Then, beside each item, indicate realistically if it is a needed, wanted, not needed, or electronic item. The next page includes a checklist to get you started. Once you have finished, re-write your list in priority order. This will keep you focused on the essentials only.

Marketing Materials Checklist

Item	Need	Want	Don't Need	Electronic
Logo				
Business Cards				
Brochure				
Website				
Newsletter				
Catalogue				
Advertisements				
Flyers				
Fridge Magnet				
Branded Swag (pens, etc.)				
Employee Clothing				
Product Labels				
Signage				
Internal Templates (Fax Cover, Memo, etc.)				
Email Signature				
Blog				
Letterhead + Envelopes				
Thank You Cards				
Notepads				
Seasonal Gifts				
Company Profile				

Headlines + Sub headlines

If your headlines were all a potential customer read, how do you think your marketing materials would fare? Headlines need to be bold, dramatic, shocking and absolutely answer the questions "What's in it for me?" or, "Why should I care?"

Headlines (and sub headlines) are vital in today's market because we are bombarded with so much information that we scan everything. Readers are skimming your materials to find out why they should bother paying attention to your product or service. Hit their hot buttons, and tell them why they should care, in your headlines!

Remember that headlines and sub headlines are not just for advertisements. They work wonders in newsletters, sales letters, brochures and websites, and can be incorporated into all of your essential marketing materials.

Design

The cost of professional design can eat up the majority of your marketing budget in a hurry. However, the cost of distributing materials that look and feel unprofessional can often be much higher. The key is to find the middle ground.

Unless you have design or desktop publishing experience – or even if you do – your time is probably not best spent designing your own marketing materials. Depending on the size of your business and your graphic needs (i.e., Do you need frequent photography of your products?) there are a number of options you can choose from:

1. **Hire a design agency.** This is no doubt the most costly of your options. However, if you have a number of items to be designed, you may be able to get a package rate. Another option is to have the design agency create a logo and stationery package for you, then create a "how-to" guide for use of the logo, fonts, and other graphic elements in the rest of your marketing materials.

2. **Hire a freelance designer.** For most small businesses, the benefits of using a freelance designer (aside from cost savings) are convenience and trust. If you are lucky enough to find one you work well with, work hard to establish a seamless working relationship and you'll never worry about the design of your marketing materials again. Ask colleagues for recommendations of local designers, or post an ad on craigslist.

3. **Hire a part-time design employee.** Need to hire someone part-time for a task around the office or shop? Consider recruiting someone with design skills and hiring them for full-time work. This could include graphic design students, or someone with an interest (and talent) in the field.

Whichever option you choose – or if you choose to design your materials yourself - the two most important things to remember about design are:

1. **Keep it consistent.** Your marketing materials must be consistent, or your customers will never learn to recognize your brand.

2. **Keep it simple.** Simple, clean design is the most effective way of communicating. Use "wow" pieces sparingly.

Guidelines for the Top 10 Marketing Materials

Logo

- **Use design resources.** If you are going to spend any money on outside design help, this is the time to do it. Your logo is the visual representation of your product or service, and appears on everything that relates to your business. This is the core of your brand image, and needs to be done right the first time.

- **Remember the purpose.** The logo needs to be a unique reflection of your business, your business values, and the industry you work in. Before you commit to your logo, make sure to give careful consideration to color choice, image selection and image recognition – as well as the logos that already exist in the marketplace. Test it out on your family and friends for an outside opinion and use their feedback.

- **Don't get too complicated.** Can it be produced (and seen clearly) in black and white? In a single color? With your company name? Too often businesses design their own logos that include a complex assortment of photos, words, and solid design elements. These do not photocopy well, and can't be clearly read at a small scale. Keep your logo design down to a graphic image and the name of your business.

Business cards

- **Cover the basics**. A business card needs to communicate your basic contact information to potential clients, including who you are and *what your business does*. Make sure you've covered the basics and made it easy for them to be in touch.

  - Name
  - Title
  - Company Name
  - Company Slogan / Description
  - Phone Number
  - Email Address
  - Fax Number
  - Address
  - Cell Number (if applicable)
  - Website

- **Make it memorable. Be creative.** Choose interesting shapes, die-cuts, orientation (vertical vs. horizontal), bright colors, and unique materials (wood, plastic, magnet, aluminum or foam). You don't have to go crazy or spend lots of money to do this – simple, clever twists on basic design make an impact. Just keep it relevant to your product or service.

- **Give them a reason to keep it.** What is going to keep them from throwing it out, or filing it in a 3" binder of other cards? Make the card worth keeping by adding something useful to the backside. For example, coffee shops put frequent buyer incentives on the backside of their cards, encouraging customers to keep them in their wallets. Other examples include pick-up schedules, reminders, calendars, testimonials, or coupons.

- **Produce a high quality card.** Use at least 100lb card stock, and print in color. Choose clear, easy to read fonts that aren't any smaller than 9pt.

Letterhead

- **Ensure a professional quality.** Letterhead that is simple, clean, and well produced allows the reader to focus on the important part: the content. Have your letterhead professionally printed on 32lb paper, or choose a textured stock. Show that you are invested in the professionalism of your company.

- **Pay attention to design choices.** The design of your marketing collateral should reflect your corporate values and the personality of your organization. If you are environmentally conscious, choose recycled paper and write it in small print at the bottom of the page. Letterhead can also be a place for subtle graphic elements, like watermarks, in addition to your logo.

- **Keep consistent with other materials.** Your letterhead is part of your stationery package, and should look and feel the same as the rest of your pieces. For example, if your business cards have been printed with rounded corners, so should your letterhead. Use consistent fonts, colors, and logo placement on your letterhead, business cards, fax cover sheets, and other internal documents to ensure recognition and ease of readability.

Brochures

- **Cover the basics.** Each brochure you produce should include your basic marketing message, USP, and detailed company contact information. Product or service features, and customer benefits should be clearly displayed and described.

- **Be purpose-focused.** Why are you producing this brochure? Are you featuring a new product line? Trying to increase awareness? Introducing your service to a new market? Stay closely connected to the purpose behind your brochure, and ensure that all of the information (and images) in the brochure support that purpose.

- **Keep it simple.** Make sure the design and information organization is clean and easy to navigate. Like advertisements, leaving blank spaces gives the reader a break and makes it easier to narrow in on key messages.

- **Choose high quality production.** If you don't invest in your business, why should anyone else? Produce your brochure on high quality paper, in vivid color, and have it professionally folded. An impressive-looking brochure will travel farther than a homemade one – from one client's hands to another's.

- **Keep it fresh.** If you produce brochures on a regular basis, consider giving each a theme to distinguish the information as new and interesting. Keep the overall look and feel consistent, but play with images and content layout to revitalize the design.

Newsletters

- **Be in touch.** Don't wait until your existing clients walk back into your store. Show them they're important to your business, and keep them updated on new products and services by keeping distributing a personalized newsletter.

- **Use an online distribution service.** Online email marketing tools (CRM tools) have never been easier or cheaper to use, and enable you to personalize your letters without much effort. They will also track for you which clients open their newsletters, and which click through to your website.

- **Provide information, tell a story.** Engage the reader with a short anecdote, or a piece of relevant information. Many people are bombarded by hard-copy and electronic letters on a daily basis, so make sure yours is worthy of their reading time. Include an "experts corner" or "new product feature" and structure the newsletter like your own business newspaper. Add links to relevant media articles, or special offers.

- **Choose a frequency you can maintain.** Newsletters can be time consuming, so be realistic about how often you promise to distribute them. This depends on your resources, and the needs of your business, but generally once a month to once every three months is a good time frame.

Company (or Corporate) Profile

- **Your ultimate company brochure.** Your company profile includes all pertinent information on your business and your offering, and acts as the base for all other marketing items. These are generally longer pieces – from five to 20 pages in length, allowing you ample room for written and visual content.

- **Tell your story.** The company profile is the place to tell the story of your business. Engage the reader, use anecdotes, and describe how and why your company was created. If you inherited the family business, describe how you're carrying on tradition and instilling new life. If you created your company from scratch with your college roommate, let the reader know. These real life details are interesting and establish trust with your potential clients and associates.

- **Communicate your values.** Here you have the space to describe your company's vision, values and approach, or philosophies. Make sure you relate your values to your offering, and keep this section short and succinct.

- **Explain your offering – features, benefits and all.** Just like your brochure, make sure to describe the full features and benefits of your product or service. Sprinkle testimonials throughout the design to back up your statements. This can include your full range of services, or simply an overview of your product types. Use professional images and creative copy to keep readers engaged.

- **Choose high-quality design and production.** Spend time creating a company profile that will last. Then, spend money producing one that will impress. Choose glossy paper, and a high-quality press, and leave the profiles around your store and office for clients to read and admire.

Signage

- **Get professional advice.** Outdoor signage can be a daunting task for anyone who hasn't designed, produced, or otherwise gone through the process. Since signage is influenced by a variety of factors – one of which is your municipal government signage bylaw – you may wish to enlist the help of a professional (a signage designer or printer) to guide you through the process and avoid costly errors.

- **Make it visible.** All of your outdoor signage should be easily seen from the street, or within the plaza or complex you are located in. In some cases, you may need more than one sign to do this. Keep in mind how your sign will look at night, as well as during the day, as your company logo and phone number or website needs to be visible at all times.

- **Make it distinct.** When it comes to signage, you can get really creative with materials, lights, and colors. While you need to maintain logo, color, and font consistency, you can add other graphic elements that may not work on the rest of your collateral, including 3D elements and window treatments. Make it memorable.

- **Remember your indoor signage.** Every business needs indoor signage to continually remind customers where they are. This includes section signage, product signage, way finding systems, and promotion announcements. If your business is located in an office, consider signage with your logo and company name above the reception area. Again, keep this signage consistent with the rest of your company materials, and you will be contributing to brand recognition.

Advertisements + Flyers

- **Place ads strategically.** Once you have determined who your target market is, you need to focus on advertising in the publications they are most likely to read, and distributing flyers in places they are most likely to be. Spend ad dollars strategically, and don't spend them all at once. Take time to test what publications work, and which don't by measuring the response from each placement. And, when you place ads, request placement that is well-forward and in the top right hand corner.

- **Grab their attention.** You have less than half a second to grab the attention of your audience with print advertising, so use it wisely. Spend the bulk of your time crafting the headline and choosing compelling images.

- **Keep their attention.** If you caught their attention, you have another two seconds to keep it. Use subheadings to further entice them to read on for the details of your product or service offer.

- **Tell them why they should buy.** Always include your marketing message or USP in your advertising. Describe the features and benefits of your product or service, but focus on the benefits that will trigger an emotional response from your target audience – love, money, luxury, convenience, and security.

- **Tell them how they can buy.** Include a call to action beside your contact information, and include your phone number, website address, and business address (if applicable). You may wish to include a scarcity or urgency offer to compel your readers to act fast.

- **Know the importance of white space.** If you try to cram too much information into your ad or flyer, your readers will skip it. Clean, clear, easy to read ads and one-page flyers with succinct messages are most effective.

Website

- **Be purpose-focused.** Like your brochure, your website can serve a number of purposes. To be effective, you need to narrow in on the specific purpose when designing the content structure of the pages. Who is your audience? What do you want them to leave the site knowing? What do you want the site to make them do? Visit your store? Buy your offering? Pick up the phone? Make sure you are clear on this point before you start.

- **Make the address easy to remember (and find!).** A website address that is too long or too complicated will not get remembered, or found. Do a search for available website addresses that relate to your business or marketing message, and try to secure a site with a

.com ending. If your company name is taken, use your USP or guarantee instead.

- **Focus on content.** The overall structure of how you organize the content on your site is like the foundation of your house. You can change the paint color, and the furniture, but the foundation is more or less there for good. Before you work with a designer and create the visual fabric of your website, focus on creating solid copy that is clearly organized. Put together a map of your structure, starting with your homepage and subpages, and allocating specific content to each page.

- **Revitalize regularly.** Your company is always changing, and so should your website. This is an important (and relatively inexpensive) way to communicate your company news and achievements, and most likely the easiest accessed source of information. Have areas for easy content updates – like a "news" section – and make sure sections like "employees" and "services" are kept up to date. For larger updates, go back to your purpose and website map, and make sure the content changes still support the original intent of the website.

- **Organize for intuition.** Make key information easy to access – especially your contact information. You can quickly tell if a website is easy to navigate, because the information you are looking for appears in a natural order. For example, when visiting a restaurant website, a link to the reservations page is provided on the menu page. While you're putting together your website map, do some research online and investigate what does and doesn't work. A good rule of thumb is to ensure it takes no more than three clicks to access a page. Bury content too deep, and your audience will get frustrated and leave.

- **Keep consistent with marketing materials.** Your website is an extension of your marketing campaign, and should be treated as such. Use consistent logo placements, fonts, colors and images so that all elements of your collateral are unified. Likewise with marketing campaigns. If you are running a new promotion, or featuring a new item in an advertisement, include that information on your website. Customers responding to the ad will be reinforced, and customers who did not see the ad will be aware of the offer.

- **Measure your results.** Your website is a piece of your marketing collateral, just like brochures and advertisements, and should be evaluated for effectiveness on a regular basis. Easy website analysis tools, like Google Analytics, will show you which pages your audience is viewing, how long they're staying on each page, and where and when they leave the site. That is powerful information when it comes to structuring content, and choosing which page to put your most important messages.

7

Profiting from Internet Marketing

Is your business online? If not, it should be.

The internet is today's primary consumer research tool. If your business does not have an online presence, it is harder for customers to find and choose your business over the competition. With over 73% of North Americans online, it is no wonder that individuals and businesses in all industries are looking to the internet to enhance their marketing strategies.

Luckily, it has never been easier to establish and maintain a comprehensive online presence. Internet marketing, also referred to as online marketing, online advertising or e-marketing, is the fastest growing medium for marketing.

But it is not just company websites that users are viewing. Blogs, consumer reviews, chat rooms and a variety of social media are growing rapidly in popularity.

The internet is a very powerful tool for businesses if used strategically and effectively. It can be a cost saving alternative to traditional marketing approaches, and may be the most effective way to communicate with your target consumer.

A major advantage of the internet is that you are always open. Users can access your business 24 hours a day, 7 days a week, and depending on your business and the purpose of the website, visitors can also purchase goods at any time.

Internet Marketing for Everyone

The internet is a great way to create product and brand awareness, develop relationships with consumers and share and exchange information. You can't afford not be taking advantage of online marketing opportunities because your competition is likely already there.

Internet marketing can take on many different forms. By creating maintaining a website for your business, you are reaching out to a new consumer base. You can have full control over the messaging that users are receiving and has a global reach.

Internet marketing can be very cost effective. If you have a strong email database of your customers, an e-newsletter may be cheaper and more effective than post mail. You can deliver time sensitive materials immediately and can update your subscribers instantaneously.

Top 10 Websites (Globally Jan 2017)

1.	Google	7.	Wikipedia
2.	Facebook	8.	Tencent QQ
3.	YouTube	9.	LinkedIn
4.	Windows Live	10.	Taobao.com
5.	Yahoo	11.	Twitter
6.	Baidu.com		

You will notice that half of these websites are search engines. An increasing number of consumers are first researching products, services and companies online, whether it be to compare products, complete a sale, or look for a future employer. Most people in the 18-35 age group obtain all of their information online—including news, weather, product research, etc. The remaining sites are interactive sites where users can upload information for social networking, or information sharing.

Internet Marketing Strategies

Internet marketing – like all other elements of your marketing campaign – needs to have clear goals and objectives. Creating brand and product awareness will not happen overnight so it is important to budget accordingly, ensuring there is money set aside for maintenance of the website and analytics.

Be flexible with ideas and options—do your research first, try out different options, then test and measure the results. Metrics and evaluations can be updated almost immediately and should be monitored regularly. By keeping an eye out for what online marketing strategies are working and which are not, it will be easier to create a balanced portfolio of marketing techniques. You might find that in certain geographical areas, certain marketing strategies are more effective than others.

This list is by no means the full extent of options available for marketing online, but it is a good place to start when deciding which options are best suited to your company.

Create a website

The primary use for the internet is information seeking, so you should provide consumers with information about your company first hand. You have more control over your branding and messaging and can also collect visitor information to determine what types of internet users are accessing your website.

Search Engine Optimization

Since search engines comprise 50% of the most visited sites globally, you can go through your website to make it more search engine friendly with the aim to increase your organic search listing. An organic search listing refers to listings in search engine results that appear in order or relevance to the entered search terms.

You may wish to repeat key words multiple times throughout your website and write the copy on your site not only with the end reader in mind, but also search engines.

Remember when you design your website that any text that appears in Flash format is not recognized by search engines. If your entire website is built on a Flash platform, then you will have a poor organic search listing.

Price Per Click Advertising

If you find that visitors access your website after searching for it first on a search engine, then it may be beneficial to advertise on these websites and bid on keywords associated with your company.

These advertisements will appear at the top of the page or along the left side of the search results on a search engine. You can have control over the specific geographic area you wish to target, set a monthly budget and have the option on only being charged when a user clicks on your link.

Online Directories

Listing your business in an online directory can be an inexpensive and effective online marketing strategy.

However, you need to be able to distinguish your company from the plethora of competitors that may exist. Likely, you will need to complement this strategy with other brand awareness campaigns.

Online Ads (i.e. banner ads on other websites)

These advertisements can have positive or negative effects based on the reputation and consumer perception of the website on which you are advertising. These ads should be treated similar to print ads you may place in local newspapers or other publications.

Online Videos

With the growing popularity of sites such as You Tube, it is evident that people love researching online and being able to find video clips of the information they are seeking. Depending on your small business, you may want to upload informational videos or tutorials about your products or services.

Blogging

Blogging can be a fun and interactive way to communicate with users. A blog is traditionally a website maintained by an individual user that has regular entries, similar to a diary. These entries can be commentary, descriptions of events, pictures, videos, and more. Companies can use blogging as a way to keep users updated on current information and allow them to post comments on your blog. If blogging is something you wish to invest in, make sure that it is regularly updated and monitored.

Top 10 Mistakes to Avoid

Failure to measure ROI

Which metrics are you using? Are your visitors actually motivated to purchase or sign up? If the benefits of your online campaign are not greater than the costs incurred, then you may wish to re-evaluate your strategy.

Poor Web Design

This can leave a poor impression of your company on the visitor. A poor design could result in frustration on the visitors' part if they are not able to easily find what they went on your site to search for and also does not build trust. If consumers do not trust your company or your website, you will not be able to complete the sale and develop a longer relationship with that customer. You also need to include privacy protection and security when building trust.

This also includes ensuring all information on the website is current and having customer service available if users are experiencing difficulty or cannot find the information they are seeking. This could be as simple as providing a 'Contact Us' email or phone number for support.

Becoming locked into an advertising strategy early

Remember your marketing mix when creating a marketing strategy and avoid putting all of your eggs in one basket. Online marketing is a very valuable tool, but depending on your business and your target markets, other marketing campaigns may be the best option for you. Especially if this is your first time making a significant investment into your online sector, you want to remain flexible and able to adapt your strategy based off feedback received by researching and analyzing different options.

Acting without researching

Similar to becoming locked into an advertising strategy early, this mistake implies not dutifully testing and researching different online marketing options. For example, if your target consumer is aged 65+ and you are spending all of your marketing efforts into creating a blogging website (where the average ages of bloggers are 18-35), then you are likely not going to have a successful campaign.

Assuming more visitors means more sales

You have to go back to your original goals and the purpose of your company. More visitors may not mean more sales if your website is used primarily for information and consumers purchase their products elsewhere.

This is also vice versa. You could have an increase in sales without an increase in unique visitors if your current consumer base is very loyal and willing to spend lots of money.

Often people will collect information online about products they wish to purchase because it is easier to compare options, but they purchase in person. Even though shopping online is becoming quite popular, people still prefer to see and feel the physical product before purchasing.

Failing to follow up with customers that purchase

Return sales can account for up to 60% of total revenue. It's no wonder that organizations are always trying to maintain loyal customers and may have customer relationship management systems in place. It is easier to get a happy customer to purchase again than it is to get a new customer to purchase once.

Not incorporating online marketing into the business plan

By ensuring that your online marketing plan is fully integrated and accurately represents your organization's overall goals and objectives, the business plan will be more comprehensive and encompassing.

Trying to discover your own best practices

It is very beneficial to use trial and error to determine the best online strategy from your company, but do not be afraid to do your research and learn from what other have already figured out. There will be many cases where someone was in a very similar position as you and they may have some suggestions and secrets that they wish to share. Researching in advance can save a great deal of time and money.

Spending too much too fast

Although it may be cheaper than traditional marketing approaches, internet marketing does have its costs. You have to consider the software and hardware designs, maintenance, distribution, supply chain management, and the time that will be required. You don't want to spend your entire marketing budget all at once.

Getting distracted by metrics that are not relevant

As discussed in the following section, there are endless reports and measurables that you can analyze to determine the effectiveness of your campaign. You will need to establish which measurables are actually relevant to your marketing.

Testing and Measuring Online

As with any element of your marketing campaign, you will need to track your results and measure them against your investment. Otherwise, how will you know if your online marketing is successful?

These results - or metrics – need to be recorded and analyzed as to how they impact your overall return on investment.

Some examples of metrics are:

- New account setups
- Conversion rates
- Page stickiness
- Contact us form completion

Due to the popularity in online marketing and the importance of having a strong web presence, companies have demanded more sophisticated tracking tools and metrics for their online activities. It can be very difficult to not only know what to measure, but also HOW to measure.

Thankfully, it is easier than ever to get the information you need with the many types of software and services available, including Google Analytics, which are free and relatively accurate.

8 Metrics to Track

The following are the key measurables to watch for when testing and measuring your internet marketing efforts:

Conversions

How many leads has your online presence generated, and of those leads, how many were turned into sales? Ultimately, your campaign needs to have a positive impact on your business.

Regardless of the specific purpose of the campaign – from lead generation and service sign-up, to blog entries – you need to know how many customers are taking the desired action in response to your efforts. Your tracking tool will be able to provide you with this information

Spend

If you are not making a profit – or at least breaking even – from your internet marketing efforts, then you need to change your strategy. Redistribute your financial resources and reconsider your motives and objectives for your online campaign.

An easy way to do this analysis is to divide your total spend by conversions. This could also be broken down by product. You could also use tracking tool and view reports on the 'per visit value of every click,' from every type of source. Your sources can include organic/search engine referrals, direct visit (i.e. person typed your web address into their address bar), or email/newsletter.

Attention

You need to keep a close eye on how much attention you are getting on your website. One of the best ways to analyze this would be to compare unique visitors to page views per visit to time on site. How many people are visiting, how many pages they are viewing, what pages they are viewing, and how much time they are spending on the site.

A unique visitor is any one person who visits the website in a given amount of time. For example, if Evelyn visits her online banking website daily for an entire month, over that one month period, she is considered to be one unique visitor (not 30 visitors).

You may also want to incorporate referring source as well – the places online that refer customers to your website. You'll be able to determine what referring sources offer the 'best' visitors.

Top Referrals

Know who is doing the best job of referring clients to your website – and note how they are doing this. Is it the prominence of the link? Positioning? Reputation of the referring company?

Understanding where the majority of your visitors are coming from will allow you focus on those types of sources when you increase your referral sites. They also allow you to gain a better understanding of your online market – and target audience.

Bounce Rate

The bounce rate is the number of people who visit the homepage of your website, but do not visit other pages. If you have a high bounce rate, you either have all the necessary information on your homepage, or you are not giving your customers a reason to click further.

In Google Analytics, view the 'content' or 'pages' report and view the column stating bounce rate.

Errors

It is very important to track the errors that visitors receive while trying to access or view your website. For example, if someone links to your website, but makes a spelling error in typing the link, your users will see an error page in their browser, and will not ultimately make it to your website.

You can also receive reports on errors that customer's make when trying to type in your website address in their browser. You may wish to buy the domains with common spelling mistakes, and link those addresses to you true homepage. This will increase overall traffic and potential conversions.

Onsite Search Terms

If you have a 'search website' function on your website, it is useful to monitor which terms users are most frequently searching. This can provide valuable insight into the user friendliness of your site and your website's navigation system. This information will be included in the traffic reporting tool.

Bailout Rates

If you provide users with the option to purchase something on your website (i.e. shopping cart), then you can track where along the purchasing process people decided not to go through with the sale.

This could be at the first step of receiving the order summary and total, or further when stating shipping options. By obtaining this information, a company can reorganize or revamp their website to make the sales process more fluid and possibly encourage more purchases.

Here are the three main questions you should be asking yourself when evaluating your website presence:

o   Who visits my website?
o   Where do visitors come from?
o   Which pages are viewed?

8

How to Use Advertising for Immediate Profits

Why do you advertise?

Seems like a silly question, doesn't it? Placing ads in newspapers and on the radio seems like a no-brainer way of growing or maintaining your business. You let a group of people know where your business is and what you sell, and you'll always have customers dropping by, right?

Sure, it's a little more complicated than that. There's your powerful offer, your strong guarantee, the placement of your headline, and how you structure your body copy.

But what I'm really trying to drill down to is *why* you chose to place *that* ad. What is the specific purpose for each advertisement you send out into the world?

Without a solid purpose – or strategy – behind each and every advertisement, it is impossible to measure what is and is not working. If you placed an ad offering 2 for 1 shampoo one week, and sales for conditioner skyrocketed, would you consider your ad successful? Absolutely not. Sales might have gone up, but the reason you placed the ad was to speed sales on shampoo, which didn't happen.

The point is that each and every advertising dollar should be spent with purpose, focused on a desired outcome and relevant to the big picture. Advertising is expensive! What's the point, unless you're making your money back and then some?

Types of Advertising

There are endless options when it comes to choosing which media to place your advertisements with. The media is a broad and complicated industry, with highly segmented readership.

This can help and hurt your advertising efforts. You have access to highly targeted audiences, but you also may spend a great deal of money on expensive advertising that your target market doesn't go near.

Here are the major types of media advertising:

Print

Print is the most common form of advertising. Ad production is relatively easy and straightforward, and placement is less expensive than broadcast advertising. We'll be focusing on this form of advertising in detail later in the chapter.

Types of print media:
Newspapers – daily and weekly
Magazines
Trade Journals
Newsletters

Radio

Radio advertising reaches a broad audience within a geographic area. This form of advertising can be highly profitable for some businesses, and utterly useless for others. Always consider if there is a simpler, cheaper way of getting your message to your target audience.

Key points to consider for radio advertising:

Use of sounds, voices, tones
Length
Gaining listener's attention
Call to action

Television

Television advertising is largely out of reach for most small business budgets. Creating, developing, and producing TV spots is a costly endeavor, and does not always generate an acceptable return on investment.

This form of advertising generally reaches a broad audience, depending on the timeslot the ad spot airs. Typically, the most expensive airspace is during the region's most popular 6 o'clock news program, or prime time (6pm to 10pm) television line-up.

There are some cost-effective alternatives to TV advertising that you can implement online. You could create a promotional video for your company, and post it on your website and YouTube, or Facebook, or play it in your store. Be creative with your ad budget when it comes to broadcast media.

Online

Online advertising has emerged as an effective tool for your marketing efforts. Internet usage has dramatically increased, and usage patterns have become easier to identify. This form of advertising also allows you to reach a highly qualified audience with minimal investment in ad creation.

Places to advertise online:

Facebook
Google Adwords
Online media (online newspapers and broadcast stations)
Craigslist
Banner ads on complementary websites

Classified

Classified advertising is one of the most highly targeted and cost-effective choices you can make in your overall strategy. People who read classifieds have typically made a decision to buy something, and are looking for places to do so. This is also a great way to test your headlines, offer, and guarantee before you invest in higher-priced advertising.

Classified ad types:

Daily and weekly newspapers
Online
Trade journals

Specific tips for effective classified ads:

- Pick a format for your ad within the specifications of the publication. Will it look like a print display ad? A semi-display ad? A classic line ad? This will affect how you structure your message.

- Choose the category – or two – that best fit with what you have to offer. If two apply, place an ad in both and measure which category generated more leads.

- Grab the attention of your reader with a killer headline, then list benefits, make an irresistible offer, and offer a strong guarantee. Keep the layout simple and ensure the font size is easy to read.

- Notice how other companies are creating their ads, and do something to stand out. The classifieds page is typically cluttered and full of text, so you will need to distinguish your business in some way.

- Use standard abbreviations when creating line ads to maintain consistency. Ask the ad department for a list of abbreviations they typically use.

Niche

Niche advertising can take any of the forms discussed above. The advantage of niche advertising is the super segmentation of each outlet's audience. Typically, there is a very small market in each niche, and a single publication that caters to it. This is very effective for companies who have no need for broad market advertising in traditional or mainstream publications.

Types of niche advertising:

> Trade journals
> Alternative media
> Online blogs
> Internal communications – newsletters, etc.

Your Advertising Strategy

Develop a strategy that is purpose driven.

Know exactly why you are choosing advertising, as well as the objective of each and every ad. Compare the benefits of advertising to other promotional strategies like media relations, direct mail, referral strategies and customer loyalty programs.

Some common objectives for advertising strategies include:

- Generate qualified leads
- Increase sales
- Promote new products or services
- Position products or services
- Increase business awareness
- Maintain business awareness
- Complement existing promotional strategies

These objectives will dictate where you advertise, how big each of your advertisements is, and how often you advertise in each outlet.

Find your target audience.

Before you do *anything*, get a solid handle on who your target market is, and each of the segments within it. Think about demographic factors like age, sex, location and occupation, as well as behavioral factors like spending motivations and habits.

The composition of your target audience will be the deciding factor when choosing which media to advertise with, and what to say in each of the advertisements.

Decide on a frequency.

The frequency of your advertising campaign will depend on a number of factors, including budget, purpose, outlet, results, and timing. You may wish to publish a weekly ad that includes a coupon in your local paper. Or, you may only need to advertise a few times a year, just before your peak seasons.

Establish an advertising schedule for the year, or at least each quarter, and plan each advertisement in advance. This will ensure you are not scrambling to place an ad at the last minute, and that each ad is part of an overall proactive strategy instead of a reactive one.

Choose your outlets.

Decide where you are going to advertise and how often in each outlet. You may wish to choose a variety of media to reach several target audiences, or just a large daily newspaper where the most number of people will see it.

It is a good idea when you are starting a new campaign to test its effectiveness in smaller, less expensive publications. Based on the results, you can make changes to the ad and place it in the more expensive outlets.

Remember that although budget is a large factor when deciding on advertising mediums, it is entirely possible to implement a successful ad campaign with minimal cost investment. The key is to make sure that each dollar you spend is carefully thought through – and that your ads are placed in publications that will reach your ideal customers.

Maximize your ad spend with bulk purchases.

If you plan to advertise in a specific publication several times in a given time period, you will benefit from a meeting with the sales representative to review your needs. Often, media outlets will offer discounted rates for multiple placements.

Remember that one company may own several media outlets – including TV, radio, and online media. Ask your sales rep for other discount opportunities when advertising within the ownership group.

Remember to test and measure

How will you know if your campaign is successful if you don't test and measure the results? The only true mistake you can make in advertising is neglecting to track and analyze the results each ad generates.

Get in the habit of keeping a copy of each ad, and record all the details of the placement, including publication, cost, date, response rate, and conversion rate. Many publications will mail you a clipping of your advertisement with your account statement, but don't rely on this as a clipping service.

Evaluate the effectiveness of each ad you place, and learn from what isn't working. If you are advertising in several outlets, make sure asking customers where they saw your ad is part of your incoming phone script and sales script. You will need to monitor not only what types of ads work the best, but also where the ads generate the highest response.

Creating Your Advertisement

You don't need to rely on professional copywriting or design assistance when crafting advertisements from your business. Spend your time and resources on what you are saying, ensure the 'how you say it' is clear, clean, and easy to read.

Ad copy

Headlines

- Take at least half of the time you spend creating your ad, and focus on the headline. Your headline will be the difference between your ad getting read – or not. Boldface your headlines for impact.

- You have about five seconds to grab the reader's attention, so create a headline that sparks curiosity, communicates benefits, or states something unbelievable.

Sub Headlines

- The purpose of your sub headline is to elaborate on your headline, and convince the audience to read the body copy. All the rules of headline writing apply. If you did not mention benefits in your headline, do it in your sub headline. Clearly tell the reader what is "in it for them," and get them reading on.

Body Copy

- Choose your words wisely – you don't have room for lengthy paragraphs. Use bullet points to convey benefits wherever possible, and keep your sentences short. You typically only have about 45 words to convince the customer to keep reading.

- Remember to always include your contact information – phone number and website address at the very least. This seems obvious, but can be forgotten in the design process.

Ad Layout

Size

- Choose your ad size based on the purpose of the ad, and the budget you have available. Larger ads are more expensive, but you do need enough space to communicate your key messages to the audience.

- If you place regular ads to maintain a presence in the local paper, you likely don't need full pages of space. Alternately, if you are launching a new product or service, or having a blowout sale, you will want to buy more space to increase the potential impact.

Graphics

- Graphics should comprise about 25% of your total ad space, and more if you have a small amount of copy. Avoid drawings and clip art. Photographs will generate a better response. Don't underestimate the importance of white space. Give the reader space to "rest" their eyes between headlines and body copy paragraphs.

Font

- Choose clean fonts that are easy to read. Times New Roman and Arial are effective, simple choices. If you use two fonts in your advertisement, make sure you do not combine serif and sans serif fonts, and you keep consistency amongst headers and body copy.

- Ensure that none of your copy is smaller than 9pt. Your audience won't take the time or spend the effort to read tiny copy.

9

How to Profit from Direct Mail

Every time you mail an existing or potential customer a letter and ask them to respond or take action, you are running a direct-mail campaign.

Direct mail is a marketing strategy that can help you achieve a number of business objectives. From lead generation to customer retention, direct mail campaigns are a highly versatile and relatively cost-effective choice for business promotion.

What you probably don't realize is that direct mail is one of the most targeted marketing strategies you can implement, and one of the easiest to track, measure and analyze results.

It is also one of the most personal. Instead of an advertisement, flyer, newspaper insert or catalogue, you are sending each customer a personalized letter that is tailored to their unique needs and desires.

Getting the most out of your direct mail campaign is easy. With a laser-sharp mailing list and irresistible offer, your direct mail campaign can easily flood your business with qualified leads.

Let's get started!

A List of Ideal Customers

Unless you spend time carefully crafting a mailing list of ideal customers, you may as well pack and up go home. The success of a direct mail campaign largely rests on the pinpoint accuracy of your mailing list.

The only people you want on your list are your potential "ideal customers." The people who are most likely to buy from you – often and in large volumes – and who are a delight to deal with. They are the type of people who will account for 80% of your revenue, and just 20% of your total customer base.

You have a number of options when you are creating your mailing list:

- **Existing customer database**. This is a list of all of the people who have previously purchased from you. It is important to gather their full contact information at the time of sale so you will be able to get contact them again.

- **Existing leads database**. This is a list of all of the leads that have come through your door, but have not purchased from you. This may include those who responded to your last direct mail campaign, but have not yet become customers.

- **Outsourced list**. This is a list that has been purchased from a market research firm, the government, or the post office. These lists are pulled based on demographic information – age, sex, location, income, family structure, etc.

Putting the mailing list together

Once you have determined the source(s) for your mailing list, you will have to spend some time assembling it and preparing it for your mailing.

1. Make sure all contacts are up to date. Phone old contacts to confirm their mailing address. An out-of-date list will cost you money in printing and postage.

2. Ensure all contacts are accurate to the list criteria. Take a read through your list to make sure there are no contacts that shouldn't be on the list.

3. Use a database management program to manage your mailing. This will allow you to keep a master list, and create custom lists for each mailing. Remember to save the file name as something that describes the mailing so you can easily find it.

Writing Effective Direct Mail Pieces

Now that you have a laser-sharp mailing list, you will want to do everything you can to target your message to the recipients on your list.

An effective direct mail piece:

- **Has a clear structure.** The piece is clearly a letter – there is an engaging headline, clear message, point form list of benefits, and postscript.

- **Features an irresistible offer.** The purchase opportunity is too good for the target audience to refuse. It includes an element of scarcity and urgency.

- **Focuses on customer benefits.** The customer clearly understands "what's in it for me?" The product or service is clearly positioned as something of value and a solution to a need, problem, or desire.

- **Is personal and conversational.** The letter is personally addressed, and reads as though it was composed specifically for the recipient. It is written in conversational tone, with short sentences and limited description.

- **Is short.** The letter communicates what it needs to, and closes. It does not go on for pages in length. The messages are clear, succinct, and simple.

- **Is urgent.** The piece gives the reader to act immediately. There is a time limit or a quantity limit to the offer that requires an urgent response.

- **Includes a Postscript.** The offer or urgency is repeated after the signature at the bottom of the letter. Like a headline, everyone will read the P.S.

The Five-Step Direct Mail Campaign

1. Determine Your Target Audience

As we discussed above, you will want to ensure that you have the most accurate, targeted list possible for your direct mail campaign.

Be clear about the purpose for your direct mail campaign – this will help you decide if you want to send your letters to your entire target market, a segment of that market, existing customers, or potentially a referring business's customers. Then you can determine how you craft your offer, how you structure your letter, and when you choose to send it.

2. Choose what you want to say

What is the message you want to communicate to your target list? What can you offer them that will entice them to act immediately?

Create a specific offer for each direct mail campaign to ensure each time you communicate with your target list you have something new to say. Tailor this offer to each mailing list.

Decide what product or service benefits will be most compelling to your target audience, and include those benefits prominently in your letter.

3. Develop a compelling direct mail piece

You are in control of how your format your message. Are you sending a letter? A brochure and a letter? A postcard? The format of your direct mail piece needs to be tailored to your target list, and reflect your product or service. A younger audience may respond to a postcard, but an older audience may appreciate a formalized letter.

Ensure that whatever format you choose, the piece is professionally designed, prominently includes your logo and company branding, and is professionally produced.

This piece of paper has to act as an ambassador of your company – you absolutely need it to appear impressive and professional.

4. Pick your timing

Some products and purchase decisions are best made at certain times of the year, or the month. If your business or service is seasonal, then there are good times and bad times to try to generate leads. Consider the best purchase windows for the people in your target marketing. When do they get paid? When do they have the money to spend on your product/service? When do they spend the most money?

Anticipate these windows, and time your direct mail campaign accordingly. If you run a lawn sprinkler installation system and summer is your peak season, run a direct mail campaign mid-way through spring, and at the beginning of summer.

Some common time windows include:

- Holiday season (November – December)
- Fridays (paydays)
- The 15th and 30th of every months (also paydays)
- Seasons (Spring, Summer, Fall, Winter)
- Financial cycles (year-end, tax time)
- Sports seasons (hockey, football, baseball, etc.)

5. Follow up

Comprehensive follow up to a direct mail campaign means two things:

1. Following up on your letter with a phone call or second letter

Often it takes more than a letter to get a potential customer to take action. This can be a result of the accuracy of your mailing list, your offer, the time of the year, or the quality of the marketing material (brochure). If you are certain that your mailing list is accurate and up to date, follow up to the piece with a phone call, or send another letter.

2. Recording, measuring and analyzing your results.

It is essential that you evaluate each direct mail campaign based on your time and financial investment and your rate of response. How else will you be able to tell if it was a successful or effective strategy?

For each campaign, record and analyze the following information:

- Number of letters sent
- Number or responses as a percentage
- Number of sales directly resulting from the campaign
- Number of enquiries
- Total value of sales directly resulting from the campaign

Based on this information, determine if the campaign was successful (did it make you money?) or not. Consider making some changes to your list, your offer, or the piece itself, and try again.

10

Profits Through Building a TEAM
(Together Everyone Achieves More)

The people you employ contribute – directly or indirectly – on a daily basis to the strength and vitality of your business. You can't run your business alone, so you rely on their skills and support.

In simpler words, your employees help you to make money.

But your employees are not just the people who arrive at your office every day and exchange effort for a paycheck. Their role is not just to build capacity and sell more or serve more.

Your employees are part of a potentially powerful group of people that you can leverage to put your business on the fast track to success. Your staff is more than the people who work for you. They are actually members of your team – the group of people who are collectively working to achieve the same objective, or reach the same vision.

I say they are more than just employees because their collective, cohesive value is actually much higher than their individual worth.

We all know that more people working on the same task will ensure the task is completed faster. In business, when you have more people working together on the same task, you save time, increase brainpower, and ultimately, **make more money**.

Corporate Culture

Corporate Culture has become a common buzzword when it comes to building a successful business, and rightly so.

Your corporate culture is the environment in which you run your business, and the environment in which your team members work. It is rooted in the vision, mission and beliefs of the organization, and dictates the "kind of office" and "kind of people" that work in that office.

Corporate culture is something that typically develops organically. The business owner and senior employees create a positive or negative environment based solely on who they are as people and how they behave as leaders. You simply can't avoid creating some type of corporate culture when you run a business.

You can, however, avoid creating a negative or unproductive corporate culture. Whether you are just starting out, or seeking to improve your workplace, you do have control over the type of environment in which you run your business.

Like most things in business, this won't happen overnight. However, with a clear idea of where you want to go, and what you want to create, you'll be well on your way to getting there.

Vision

Your company's vision statement should be a bold, clear, short sentence that every single one of your employees knows and understands. It is a roadmap to your idea of success; if you don't know what that looks like, how will you know when you achieve it?

If your goal is to create a highly profitable company – what does highly profitable mean? $1 million in annual sales?$3 million in annual profit?

Do you seek to become the industry leader in sprocket production? How will this be measured? How many sprockets will you have to produce to reach this goal?

The vision statement is a short summary of the long-term objective of the company. What the company will look like, produce, achieve; it is how you know the company is "successful."

Many companies either do not have a vision statement or they keep it a secret from their employees. It is only discussed in board meetings or management meetings. For a team to collectively work toward a goal, they need to know what the big picture objective is. They need to have buy-in in the company's direction, and be communicated with on a regular basis.

Be proud of your vision. Keep it visible for staff – post it on the wall, include it in internal communications, and connect day to day activities too it as often as possible.

Sample Vision Statements

Here are some real examples of corporate vision statements:

"At Microsoft, our mission and values are to help people and businesses through the world realize their potential." – Microsoft

"Give every customer a reason to believe...STAPLES Business Depot—That was easy!" – Staples Canada

"To build the largest and most complete Amateur Radio community site on the Internet." – eHam.net

Creating a Vision Statement

The process of creating a vision statement is something that you can work through alone, or in collaboration with your team. It is highly recommended to review the draft vision statement with your employees to ensure they understand and support the goals and objectives of the company.

Keep the following points in mind when crafting your vision statement:

- **Think big** – Why did you start or buy this business? What was your dream or purpose in doing so?
- **Think long-term** – Vision statements should last five to 10 or even 25 years
- **Be specific** – Use numbers, dates, ratings systems and other ways of

measuring success

- **Be succinct** – Use clear, short, simple sentences that are easy to repeat and remember

Mission

Your mission statement is a general description of how you are going to achieve your vision. This is a longer and more detailed statement that should include what your business is, who your customers are, and how you are different from (better than!) the competition.

Sample Mission Statements

"The Mission of McGill University is the advancement of learning through teaching, scholarship and service to society: by offering to outstanding undergraduate and graduate students the best education available; by carrying out scholarly activities judged to be excellent when measured against the highest international standards; and by providing service to society in those ways for which we are well-suited by virtue of our academic strengths." – McGill University, Montreal, Canada

"Starbucks purchases and roasts high-quality whole bean coffees and sells them along with fresh, rich-brewed, Italian style espresso beverages, a variety of pastries and confections, and coffee-related accessories and equipment -- primarily through its company-operated retail stores. In addition to sales through our company-operated retail stores, Starbucks sells whole bean coffees through a specialty sales group and supermarkets. Additionally, Starbucks produces and sells bottled

Frappuccino® coffee drink and a line of premium ice creams through its joint venture partnerships and offers a line of innovative premium teas produced by its wholly owned subsidiary, Tazo Tea Company. The Company's objective is to establish Starbucks as the most recognized and respected brand in the world." – Starbucks

Creating Your Mission Statement:

Here is a recommended process for completing your mission statement:

Step One: List your company's core strengths and weaknesses; what do you do well? What do you need to work on, or avoid doing?

Step Two: Who are your primary customers? Describe the types of customers you serve – both internal and external.

Step Three: What do your customers think of your strengths? What strengths are most important to them? Go ahead and ask them if you need to.

Step Four: Connect the strength that each customer values with its customer type. Write it in a sentence. Combine any redundancies.

Step Five: Organize your sentences in order of importance

Step Six: Combine your sentences into a paragraph or two. Elaborate on points as needed. This is your draft mission statement.

Step Six: Consult with your staff and customers, and ask for their feedback. Do employees support the statement? Can they act on it? Do customers want to do business with a company with this mission statement? Does it make sense?

Step Seven: Incorporate the feedback received, and refine the statement until you are happy with it. Then publish it – everywhere.

Culture or Values Statements

Your culture or values statement is the next step in the process. It describes how you and your staff will go about taking action (your mission statement) to achieve your objective (your vision statement).

Much like every family has their own belief system and way of doing things – from cooking to cleaning to raising kids – every company has their own set of values when it comes to running a business. It reflects the unique personality of the organization.

Sample Culture Statement

Our Culture
* Values-based leadership. Our Credo outlines the values that provide the foundation of how we act as a corporation and as individual employees so that we continue to put the needs of the people we serve first.

* Diversity. It's our individual differences that make us stronger as a whole. We recognize the strength and value that comes when collaborative

relationships are built between people of different ages, race, gender, religion, nationality, sexual orientation, physical ability, thinking style, personal backgrounds and all other attributes that make each person unique.

* Innovation. True innovation can only be fostered within a supportive environment that values calculated risk in order to achieve the maximum reward. At Johnson & Johnson Inc., we encourage and reward innovative thinking, innovative solutions and an innovative approach in all that we do.

* Passion. The deep desire to enrich people's lives – by delivering quality products and remarkable experiences that make their lives easier, healthier and more joyful.

* Collaboration. The unwavering belief that great results depend on the ability to create trusting relationships.

* Courage. The fearless pursuit of the unproven, unknown possibility – the willingness to take great risks for the benefit of the greater good.

- Johnson & Johnson Canada

Creating Your Culture Statement

Involve your team in creating your company's culture or values statement. Generally, this is a point-form document that reflects the beliefs of the company, its employees, and its customers.

It can be helpful to think about the type of people you currently employ, as well as the ones you may wish to employ. What are they like? What are their belief systems? What are their most important values?

Remember that the culture or values statement is usually the longest of the three statements – and that's okay.

Your Team Leaders

The strength of a team lies in the strength of the people who lead it. No group of people is effective without strong leadership, just like no business is effective without a strong owner or management team.

Building a strong team means knowing who your leaders are – both in job description and natural ability.

Understanding the strength of your natural leaders and the skills of your natural followers will allow you to strategically structure your team for maximum effectiveness and efficiency. It will give you insight into who is best suited for management promotions and project management; which team members have the ability to assemble and motivate their peers.

Your leaders need to have a high degree of passion for your product or service, and truly believe in the company's vision. They need to be able to handle a high level of responsibility, and manage a range of people to achieve a common goal.

Your leaders are your team builders. They present new ideas, build consensus, and encourage the involvement of others.

Types of Leaders

Simply speaking, there are four main types, or styles, of leaders. Chances are, you've experienced each type at some point in your career.

Type	Description	Ideal Use
Autocratic	Classical or "old-school" approach Manager holds all power and decision-making authority No employee consultation or input Orders are obeyed Rewards/punishment structure	New, untrained employees Detailed orders and instructions are required No other leadership style has been effective Limited time available Department restructuring High production requirements
Bureaucratic	"By the book" approach All is done to specific procedures/policies All tasks outside policies referred to higher management	Routine tasks performed Standards and procedures need to be communicated regularly Safety or training Cash handling Dangerous equipment
Laissez-faire	"Hands-off" approach Employees have almost total freedom Little direction or guidance is provided Employees must make own decisions, set own goals Employees must solve own problems	Highly skilled and experienced employees Employees are highly driven and ambitious Consultants are being managed Employees are trustworthy

Democratic	"Participatory approach" Employees part of decision making process Employees well informed Leader has final say, but involved others Collaborative approach Encourages employee development with guidance and assistance from leader Leader recognizes and rewards achievement	Collaborative environment Employee development and growth is the focus Changes or problems affect employees and require their input to create a solution Team building and participation is encouraged

Communication

The only way to build and maintain a strong team is through strong, consistent communication. This is often an overlooked or neglected aspect of business management, and is easily forgotten during periods of high stress or heavy workload.

Avoid letting communication fall on the backburner by creating a regular meeting schedule – and sticking to it. Depending on the size and type of your business, daily, weekly, or monthly team meetings are an important cornerstone of a strong team.

Regularly scheduled team meetings are like Sunday dinners with a busy family. They give you – the owner – a regular forum with your staff to implement company-wide training initiatives, announce results, establish goals and targets, or share new visions or directions. They also give your staff a forum to share feedback and air grievances.

Effective Team Meetings

By now you're probably thinking, "Sure, I hear some company's team meetings are effective, but we tried them and it didn't work," or "I held regular team meetings, but after a while, no one showed up."

There is a difference between team meetings held for the sake of having team meetings, and well prepared team meetings with a purpose.

You need to start holding team meetings with a purpose.

Establish a Schedule That Everyone Can Commit To

Scheduling is potentially the biggest challenge when trying to set up a team meeting. Often, all of your staff members are busy going in eight different directions to fulfill their roles and operating on dramatically different schedules.

This is one reason why regular team meetings are important. Ad hoc meetings require ad hoc scheduling, and reduce the likelihood that all your team members will be able to attend.

Ask your team to block off one hour (or two) each week (or month) for the team meeting in a time slot that is convenient for everyone. Establish a clear attendance expectation from everyone. This will exclude that time slot from the scheduling of other meetings and avoid conflict.

If you find that a team meeting is not necessary one week, you can always cancel it.

Know Your Purpose

Each team meeting should have a purpose and clear objectives. Is it to educate? Build consensus? Gather feedback?

Once you have established a purpose for a particular meeting, send an agenda to your staff confirming the meeting and outlining your objectives. This is a good time to ask if anyone has a subject they would like to raise at the meeting.

If you find you do not have a clear purpose or objective, ask yourself if a team meeting is the best use of time for that week and consider postponing it to the next regularly scheduled time slot.

Plan Each and Every Minute

The biggest complaint from employees about team meetings is the length. Too often team meetings run out of control, and end up taking three hours instead of one. You will quickly lose team focus and respect for the regular meeting this way. By establishing a clear agenda and staying on topic, you can run an efficient, succinct meeting.

Your detailed agenda should include:

- meeting purpose or objective
- list of topics and associated speakers
- list of decisions that need to be made/agreed to
- time allocation for each topic
- opportunity for additional topics at the end

Circulate your draft agenda in advance of the meeting, and request input and feedback. When all team members have reviewed and contributed to the agenda, you will increase their level of ownership and buy-in into the process.

Establish the Facilitator

Choose one person to chair the meeting and keep it on track. This is generally the business owner or a senior member of the team with some authority over junior staff and a high level of respect.

It is the responsibility of the facilitator – or chairperson – to create an environment of open dialogue and trust, and to keep the meeting on schedule.

Create a Follow-up Schedule

Assign the task of taking detailed meeting minutes to a team member – or rotate this responsibility on a regular basis. It is important to record what happens in team meetings, just as you would in a client-related business meeting.

In the minutes, establish a system for tracking the action items that arise from decisions made in the meeting. This can be set up as a simple chart:

Decision	Action	Responsibility	Deadline

Make sure that these responsibilities are assigned and agreed upon in the meeting, and clear deadlines are established. Reviewing or following up on this chart can serve as a regular topic during team meetings.

Circulate meeting minutes to all attendees and ask for input or revisions. You may wish to circulate meeting minutes with the agenda for the next team meeting, and gather feedback at the same time.

Motivations + Incentives

A big challenge in team building is coming up with new ways to foster and maintain a high level of motivation. How do you keep teams of people excited and driven to succeed over long periods of time? How do you keep your team motivated to improve their performance, and increase their achievements?

It is important to note that we're not just talking about individuals, but teams of people working together. It is fairly simple to motivate a single person, but an entire team of motivated people will generate significantly higher results.

The key here is to give incentives for individual and team accomplishments. Incentives that reward based on collective achievement require people to work together and motivate each other to succeed.

Before we start talking about monetary and incentive-based rewards, it's important to look at motivational factors that are not incentive-driven.

Room to Work

Employees who feel their managers and supervisors believe and trust in their abilities are happier and will always perform at a higher level than those who do not. They are motivated to "prove them right" and feel supported in their efforts.

Micromanagement quickly reduces morale. It is essential that you and your managers clearly express confidence in your team members. You hired them to do a job, perform a role, so you must ensure they have the space to do so.

When you put effective systems in place and establish clear expectations, you create a clear context or boundary system for employees to work within. They understand the decision-making hierarchy, and the general way 'things are done around here.'

Your team should be encouraged to take initiative and to take risks within this context. You have hired your team based on their skills and intellectual capabilities, and thus should be able to trust in their choices and decision making abilities.

Incentives

Incentives are great motivators. An incentive is a reason to perform or act in a certain way. For example, if your team increases sales by 40% by month's end, they will be treated to an expensive dinner.

Incentives need to be specific and have deadlines in order to be effective. In the example above, sales need to increase by 40% by the end of the month in order for the team to receive their dinner. If sales only increase by 30%, or if they increase by 40% at the end of the second month, the team does not earn their reward.

Time-specific incentives increase the sense of urgency, and encourage staff to work harder to achieve the objective. If the incentive is not time-bound, there is no reason to work faster or harder, since staff will assume they will reach their milestone "eventually."

Rarity is also a key component of effective incentive-based team building. If the reward is ongoing (i.e., if staff receive an expensive dinner every month sales are over $75,000), then "there's always next time." There is a lesser incentive to push performance to receive the reward. Some team members may care one month, but not the next.

Monetary Incentives

Bonuses and salary increases are a popular way to give your team an incentive to perform. These can include:

- Commissions
- Bonuses for completing a challenging project, or hitting a target
- Rewards for highest producing employee
- Salary increases based on met targets

It's up to you how you choose to structure your monetary incentives, based on your budget and resources. Remember to ensure that the terms of each incentive are clearly outlined, and that both parties (you and your employee) understand the agreement.

Gift Rewards

Physical, tangible gifts are an inexpensive way to reward your team for achievements and improvement. These rewards show that you have given some level of thought to what they might enjoy or appreciate in exchange for a job well done. They're also a great way to surprise employees.

Here are some ideas:

- Spa gift certificates
- Books – *consider motivational or business-related topics*
- CDs or DVDs
- Meals – lunch or breakfast
- Other gift certificates – gas, food, meals, local shops
- Movie or theatre tickets
- Weekend getaway – hotel, meals, etc.
- Flowers
- Gym memberships

So What Do You Do From Here?

Take Action! If you're already an accomplished business owner and earning in excess of $250,000.00 per year (rich according to the Federal Government), use this book as direction to enhance the speed of your business success. If you are not as accomplished as you would like to be then the smartest thing to do is...

A) Generate and Convert Your Leads
B) Make your Website Work for You
C) Add Value to Gain More Profits

Concentrate on strategies to LEARN and the EARN will follow! If you are serious about taking the next step then go to work on yourself, study other business successes, understand marketing strategies and become a sponge for new (proven) material. The amazing thing about the game of business is that when you put proven processes to work and continue to follow them, an abundance of success will follow. The biggest mistake is to start a process and then fallback into your old habits after a short time.

Above all, get the knowledge you need before you step onto the field. Think about it... if you were going to challenge Roger Federer to a game of tennis for money, wouldn't it make sense to learn the game and practice before you stepped on the court to play him? It is amazing to me how many new small business people start the game of business against seasoned professionals (the competition), without first developing the necessary knowledge to be successful. Then they fail and blame the market, the economy, their location, etc.

If you have a business and have not yet managed to start to create wealth and systems that allow you to take time off, build retirement accounts or pay for your children's college, then learn and master the steps outlined in my book. I am a huge advocate of education and mentorships. Get the right information, find someone that knows how to walk you through them and watch your quality of life take new shape.

To learn how to avoid the 3 key mistakes all small business owners make, visit www.smallbusinessrocks.us (your membership site)